Microsoft

MOS Study Guide for Microsoft Word Expert Exam MO-101

Paul McFedries

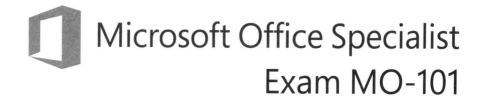Microsoft Office Specialist
Exam MO-101

MOS Study Guide for Microsoft Word Expert Exam MO-101

Published with the authorization of Microsoft Corporation by:
Pearson Education, Inc.

ISBN-13: 978-0-13-662837-8
ISBN-10: 0-13-662837-0

Library of Congress Control Number: 2020933986

1 2020

Trademarks
Microsoft and the trademarks listed at http://www.microsoft.com on the
"Trademarks" webpage are trademarks of the Microsoft group of companies. All
other marks are property of their respective owners.

Warning and Disclaimer
Every effort has been made to make this book as complete and as accurate as
possible, but no warranty or fitness is implied. The information provided is on
an "as is" basis. The author, the publisher, and Microsoft Corporation shall have
neither liability nor responsibility to any person or entity with respect to any loss
or damages arising from the information contained in this book or from the use of
the programs accompanying it.

Special Sales
For information about buying this title in bulk quantities, or for special sales
opportunities (which may include electronic versions; custom cover designs;
and content particular to your business, training goals, marketing focus, or
branding interests), please contact our corporate sales department at
corpsales@pearsoned.com or (800) 382-3419.

For government sales inquiries, please contact governmentsales@pearsoned.com.

For questions about sales outside the U.S., please contact intlcs@pearson.com.

Editor-in-Chief
Brett Bartow

Executive Editor
Loretta Yates

Development Editor
Songlin Qiu

Managing Editor
Sandra Schroeder

Senior Project Editor
Tracey Croom

Sponsoring Editor
Charvi Arora

Copy Editor
Elizabeth Welch

Indexer
Cheryl Ann Lenser

Proofreader
Abigail Manheim

Technical Editor
Boyd Nolan

Editorial Assistant
Cindy Teeters

Cover Designer
Twist Creative, Seattle

Compositor
codeMantra

Contents

Introduction

The Microsoft Office Specialist (MOS) certification program has been designed to validate your knowledge of and ability to use programs in the Microsoft Office 365 and Microsoft Office 2019 suite of programs. This book has been designed to guide you in studying the types of tasks you are likely to be required to demonstrate in Exam MO-101, "Microsoft Word Expert (Word and Word 2019)."

◇◇

Exam Strategy For information about the tasks you are likely to be required to demonstrate in the core Word exam, Exam MO-100, "Microsoft Word (Word and Word 2019)," see *MOS Study Guide for Microsoft Word Exam MO-100* by Joan Lambert (Microsoft Press, 2020).

◇◇

Who this book is for

MOS Study Guide for Microsoft Word Expert Exam MO-101 is designed for experienced computer users seeking Microsoft Office Specialist Expert certification in Word 365 and Word 2019.

MOS exams for individual programs are practical rather than theoretical. You must demonstrate that you can complete certain tasks or projects rather than simply answer questions about program features. The successful MOS certification candidate will have at least six months of experience using all aspects of the program on a regular basis—for example, creating and modifying styles, building and inserting indexes and reference tables, customizing themes and style sets, protecting a document, and using advanced page setup options.

As a certification candidate, you probably have a lot of experience with the program you want to become certified in. Many of the procedures described in this book will be familiar to you; others might not be. Read through each study section and ensure that you are familiar with the procedures, concepts, and tools discussed. In some cases, images depict the tools you will use to perform procedures related to the skill set. Study the images and ensure that you are familiar with the options available for each tool.

How this book is organized

The exam coverage is divided into chapters representing broad skill sets that correlate to the functional groups covered by the exam. Each chapter is divided into sections addressing groups of related skills that correlate to the exam objectives. Each section includes review information, generic procedures, and practice tasks you can complete on your own while studying. We provide practice files you can use to work through the practice tasks, and result files you can use to check your work. You can practice the generic procedures in this book by using the practice files supplied or by using your own files.

Throughout this book, you will find Exam Strategy tips that present information about the scope of study that is necessary to ensure that you achieve mastery of a skill set and are successful in your certification effort.

Download the practice files

Before you can complete the practice tasks in this book, you need to copy the book's practice files and result files to your computer. Download the compressed (zipped) folder from the following page, and extract the files from it to a folder (such as your Documents folder) on your computer:

MicrosoftPressStore.com/MOSWordExpert101/downloads

IMPORTANT The Word 365 and Word 2019 programs are not available from this website. You should purchase and install one of those programs before using this book.

You will save the completed versions of practice files that you modify while working through the practice tasks in this book. If you later want to repeat the practice tasks, you can download the original practice files again.

The following table lists the practice files provided for this book.

Folder and objective group	Practice files	Result files
MOSWordExpert2019\ Objective1 Manage document options and settings	WordExpert_1-1a.docx WordExpert_1-1b.docx WordExpert_1-1c.docx WordExpert_1-2.docx WordExpert_1-3.docx	WordExpert_1-1a_results.docx WordExpert_1-1c_results.docx WordExpert_1-2_results.docx
MOSWordExpert2019\ Objective2 Use advanced editing and formatting features	WordExpert_2-1.docx WordExpert_2-2.docx WordExpert_2-3.docx	WordExpert_2-1_results.docx WordExpert_2-2_results.docx WordExpert_2-3_results.docx
MOSWordExpert2019\ Objective3 Create custom document elements	WordExpert_3-1.docx WordExpert_3-2a.docx WordExpert_3-2b.docx WordExpert_3-3a.docx WordExpert_3-3b.docx WordExpert_3-3c.docx WordExpert_3-4.docx	WordExpert_3-2a_results.docx WordExpert_3-2b_results.docx WordExpert_3-3a_results.docx WordExpert_3-3b_results.docx WordExpert_3-3c_results.docx WordExpert_3-4_results.docx
MOSWordExpert2019\ Objective4 Use advanced Word features	WordExpert_4-1a.docx WordExpert_4-1b.docx WordExpert_4-2.docm WordExpert_4-3.docx WordExpert_4-3.xlsx	WordExpert_4-1a_results.docx WordExpert_4-1b_results.docx WordExpert_4-2_results.docm WordExpert_4-3_results.docx

Adapt procedure steps

This book contains many images of user interface elements that you'll work with while performing tasks in Word on a Windows computer. Depending on your screen resolution or program window width, the Word ribbon on your screen might look different from that shown in this book. (If you turn on Touch mode, the ribbon displays significantly fewer commands than in Mouse mode.) As a result, procedural instructions that involve the ribbon might require a little adaptation.

Simple procedural instructions use this format:

→ On the **Insert** tab, in the **Illustrations** group, click the **Pictures** button.

If the command is in a list, our instructions use this format:

→ On the **Home** tab, in the **Editing** group, click **Find & Select** and then, in the **Find & Select** list, click **Go To**.

If differences between your display settings and ours cause a button to appear differently on your screen than it does in this book, you can easily adapt the steps to locate the command. First click the specified tab, and then locate the specified group. If a group has been collapsed into a group list or under a group button, click the list or button to display the group's commands. If you can't immediately identify the button you want, point to likely candidates to display their names in ScreenTips.

The instructions in this book assume that you're interacting with on-screen elements on your computer by clicking (with a mouse, touchpad, or other hardware device). If you're using a different method—for example, if your computer has a touchscreen interface and you're tapping the screen (with your finger or a stylus)—substitute the applicable tapping action when you interact with a user interface element.

Instructions in this book refer to user interface elements that you click or tap on the screen as *buttons*, and to physical buttons that you press on a keyboard as *keys*, to conform to the standard terminology used in documentation for these products.

Ebook edition

If you're reading the ebook edition of this book, you can do the following:

- Search the full text
- Print
- Copy and paste

You can purchase and download the ebook edition from the Microsoft Press Store at:

MicrosoftPressStore.com/MOSWordExpert101/detail

Errata, updates, & book support

We've made every effort to ensure the accuracy of this book and its companion content. If you discover an error, please submit it to us through the link at:

MicrosoftPressStore.com/MOSWordExpert101/errata

For additional book support and information, please visit:

www.MicrosoftPressStore.com/Support

For help with Microsoft software and hardware, go to:

https://support.microsoft.com

Stay in touch

Let's keep the conversation going! We're on Twitter at:

https://twitter.com/MicrosoftPress

Taking a Microsoft Office Specialist exam

Desktop computing proficiency is increasingly important in today's business world. When screening, hiring, and training employees, employers can feel reassured by relying on the objectivity and consistency of technology certification to ensure the competence of their workforce. As an employee or job seeker, you can use technology certification to prove that you already have the skills you need to succeed, saving current and future employers the time and expense of training you.

Microsoft Office Specialist certification

Microsoft Office Specialist certification is designed to assist students and information workers in validating their skills with Office programs. The following certification paths are available:

- A Microsoft Office Specialist (MOS) is an individual who has demonstrated proficiency by passing a certification exam in one or more Office programs, including Microsoft Word, Excel, PowerPoint, Outlook, or Access.

- A Microsoft Office Specialist Expert (MOS Expert) is an individual who has taken his or her knowledge of Office to the next level and has demonstrated by passing Core and Expert certification exams that he or she has mastered the more advanced features of Word or Excel.

- A Microsoft Office Specialist Master (MOS Master) is an individual who has demonstrated a broader knowledge of Office skills by passing the Word Core and Expert exams, the Excel Core and Expert exams, the PowerPoint exam, and the Access or Outlook exam.

Selecting a certification path

When deciding which certifications you would like to pursue, assess the following:

- The program and program version(s) with which you are familiar
- The length of time you have used the program and how frequently you use it
- Whether you have had formal or informal training in the use of that program
- Whether you use most or all of the available program features
- Whether you are considered a go-to resource by business associates, friends, and family members who have difficulty with the program

Candidates for MOS certification are expected to successfully complete a wide range of standard business tasks. Successful candidates generally have six or more months of experience with the specific Office program, including either formal, instructor-led training or self-study using MOS-approved books, guides, or interactive computer-based materials.

Candidates for MOS Expert and MOS Master certification are expected to successfully complete more complex tasks that involve using the advanced functionality of the program. Successful candidates generally have at least six months, and might have several years, of experience with the programs, including formal, instructor-led training or self-study using MOS-approved materials.

Test-taking tips

Every MOS certification exam is developed from a set of exam skill standards (referred to as the *objective domain*) that are derived from studies of how the Office programs are used in the workplace. Because these skill standards dictate the scope of each exam, they provide critical information about how to prepare for certification. This book follows the structure of the published exam objectives.

See Also For more information about the book structure, see "How this book is organized" in the Introduction.

The MOS certification exams are performance based and require you to complete business-related tasks in the program for which you are seeking certification. For example, you might be presented with a document and told to insert and format additional document elements. Your score on the exam reflects how many of the requested tasks you complete within the allotted time.

Here is some helpful information about taking the exam:

- Keep track of the time. Your exam time does not officially begin until after you finish reading the instructions provided at the beginning of the exam. During the exam, the amount of time remaining is shown in the exam instruction window. You can't pause the exam after you start it.

- Pace yourself. At the beginning of the exam, you will receive information about the tasks that are included in the exam. During the exam, the number of completed and remaining tasks is shown in the exam instruction window.

- Read the exam instructions carefully before beginning. Follow all the instructions provided completely and accurately.

- If you have difficulty performing a task, you can restart it without affecting the result of any completed tasks, or you can skip the task and come back to it after you finish the other tasks on the exam.

- Enter requested information as it appears in the instructions, but without duplicating the formatting unless you are specifically instructed to do so. For example, the text and values you are asked to enter might appear in the instructions in bold and underlined text, but you should enter the information without applying these formats.

- Close all dialog boxes before proceeding to the next exam item unless you are specifically instructed not to do so.

- Don't close task panes before proceeding to the next exam item unless you are specifically instructed to do so.

- If you are asked to print a document, worksheet, chart, report, or slide, perform the task, but be aware that nothing will actually be printed.

- Don't worry about extra keystrokes or mouse clicks. Your work is scored based on its result, not on the method you use to achieve that result (unless a specific method is indicated in the instructions).

- If a computer problem occurs during the exam (for example, if the exam does not respond or the mouse no longer functions) or if a power outage occurs, contact a testing center administrator immediately. The administrator will restart the computer and return the exam to the point where the interruption occurred, with your score intact.

◇◇

Exam Strategy This book includes special tips for effectively studying for the Microsoft Office Specialist exams in Exam Strategy paragraphs such as this one.

◇◇

Certification benefits

At the conclusion of the exam, you will receive a score report, indicating whether you passed the exam. If your score meets or exceeds the passing standard (the minimum required score), you will be contacted by email by the Microsoft Certification Program team. The email message you receive will include your Microsoft Certification ID and links to online resources, including the Microsoft Certified Professional site. On this site, you can download or order a printed certificate, create a virtual business card, order an ID card, review and share your certification transcript, access the Logo Builder, and access other useful and interesting resources, including special offers from Microsoft and affiliated companies.

Depending on the level of certification you achieve, you will qualify to display one of three logos on your business card and other personal promotional materials. These logos attest to the fact that you are proficient in the applications or cross-application skills necessary to achieve the certification. Using the Logo Builder, you can create a personalized certification logo that includes the MOS logo and the specific programs in which you have achieved certification. If you achieve MOS certification in multiple programs, you can include multiple certifications in one logo.

For more information

To learn more about the Microsoft Office Specialist exams and related courseware, visit:

http://www.certiport.com/mos

About the Author

Paul McFedries is a Word expert and full-time technical writer. Paul has been authoring computer books since 1991 and has nearly 100 books to his credit, which combined have sold more than 4 million copies worldwide. His titles include the Microsoft Press Publishing book *Formulas and Functions for Microsoft Excel 2019*, the Que Publishing books *My Office 2016*, *My Office for iPad*, *Windows 10 In Depth* (with coauthor Brian Knittel), and *PCs for Grownups*. Please drop by Paul's personal website at www.mcfedries.com or follow Paul on Twitter at twitter.com/paulmcf.

Microsoft Office Specialist

Exam MO-101

Microsoft Word Expert (Word and Word 2019)

This book covers the skills you need to have for certification as a Microsoft Office Specialist Expert in Microsoft Word 365 and Microsoft Word 2019. Specifically, you need to be able to complete tasks that demonstrate the following skill sets:

1. Manage document options and settings
2. Use advanced editing and formatting features
3. Create custom document elements
4. Use advanced Word features

With these skills, you can create, manage, and distribute documents for a variety of specialized purposes and situations. You can also customize your Word environment to enhance the productivity you need to work with advanced documents used in a business environment.

Prerequisites

We assume that you have been working with Word 2019 for at least six months and that you know how to carry out fundamental tasks that are not specifically mentioned in the objectives for these Microsoft Office Specialist Expert exams.

The certification exams and the content of this book address the processes of managing, designing, and customizing Word documents and managing the options and settings that Word provides. We assume that you are familiar with the Office ribbon and that you understand basic Word features. This level of proficiency includes familiarity with features and tasks such as the following:

- Creating blank documents and documents based on templates
- Navigating through documents, including searching for text, inserting hyper-links, and using the Go To command to find specific objects and references
- Formatting documents and text, including changing document themes, inserting simple headers and footers, and changing font attributes
- Inserting page, column, and section breaks
- Changing document views
- Printing documents, including printing document sections
- Customizing the Quick Access Toolbar
- Saving documents in alternate file formats
- Working with tables and lists, including using Quick Tables, applying styles to tables, and sorting table data
- Creating simple references such as footnotes and endnotes
- Inserting and formatting objects such as shapes, SmartArt, and pictures

Exam Strategy For information about the prerequisite tasks, see MOS Study Guide for Microsoft Word Exam MO-100 by Joan Lambert (Microsoft Press, 2020).

Objective group 1

Manage document options and settings

The skills tested in this section of the Microsoft Office Specialist Expert exam for Microsoft Word 365 and Microsoft Word 2019 relate to managing document options and settings. Specifically, the following objectives are associated with this set of skills:

- 1.1 Manage documents and templates
- 1.2 Prepare documents for collaboration
- 1.3 Use and configure language options

In today's work environment, you often collaborate with coworkers and colleagues to write, revise, and finalize documents. Sharing documents within a group of users often entails specific requirements and tasks. You might need to track changes that reviewers make to a document, for example, or you might have to merge copies of a document that reviewers revised independently. In some cases, documents require the protection that a password provides so that only people with the password can open and modify the file. In preparing a document to use in a collaborative process, you might need to restrict who can edit specific sections of the document.

This chapter guides you in studying ways to manage documents and templates, prepare documents for collaboration, and configure language options.

> To complete the practice tasks in this chapter, you need the practice files contained in the **MOSWordExpert2019\Objective1** practice file folder. For more information, see "Download the practice files" in this book's Introduction.

Objective 1.1: Manage documents and templates

This topic covers a range of features that you use to manage documents and templates. It describes how to modify a template, compare and combine documents, and link to external data from a document. It also describes how to manage versions of a document, customize the Quick Access toolbar, display hidden ribbon tabs, and set the default font that Word uses when you create a document from the Normal template.

Modify existing document templates

One purpose of a template is to give related documents a common look and feel. Templates provide style definitions and can contain elements such as cover pages, custom headers and footers, themes, and macros. The components of a template help you create a document that meets a defined specification without having to design the document from scratch.

To modify a Word template that you created or that you downloaded from the Start screen or the New page of the Backstage view, you first open the template file. After you open the template, you can modify it by creating styles, changing the properties of existing styles, designing custom headers or footers, and making similar types of changes.

Templates that you create are stored by default in the Custom Office Templates folder, which is a subfolder of your Documents folder. (Word opens the Custom Office Templates folder automatically when you select *Word Template* in the Save As Type list.) Templates that you download are saved in the AppData folder in your user profile. You can open this folder from File Explorer by entering **%UserProfile%\AppData\ Roaming\Microsoft\Templates** in the address bar.

IMPORTANT %UserProfile% is an environment variable that represents the top-level folder of your Windows user account. For example, if your username is Biff and Windows is installed on drive C, then the %UserProfile% environment variable value is C:\Users\Biff.

You can also modify a template when you are working on a document that is based on that template. For example, you can design a cover page for that template and then save that cover page as a building block. If you modify a template style while working in a document, you can apply the change only to the current document or to the template.

See Also For more information about working with building blocks, see "Objective 3.1: Create and modify building blocks." For more information about working with styles, see "Objective 2.3: Create and manage styles."

Select New Documents Based On This Template to include style modifications in the template.

To open an existing template for modification

1. From the **Open** page of the Backstage view, browse to the folder where the template is saved (such as the Custom Office Templates folder or the Templates folder in the AppData folder of your user profile).

2. Select the template you want to modify.

3. Click **Open**.

Or

1. Open File Explorer.

2. Browse to the folder where the template is stored.

3. Right-click the template, then click **Open**.

To modify an existing template

1. Open the template.

2. Make the changes you want to the template's styles and other elements.

3. Save and close the file.

To update a document's template while modifying a style in the document

1. On the **Home** tab, in the **Styles** group, right-click the style you want to work with, then click **Modify**.

2. In the **Modify Style** dialog box, modify the style as required.

3. Select **New Documents Based On This Template**, then click **OK**.

4. Save the document, and then click **Yes** when Word prompts you to save changes to the document template.

Manage document versions

Word uses its AutoRecover feature to save versions of a document as you write, insert content, and edit the document. You set the options related to automatically saving and recovering files on the Save page of the Word Options dialog box.

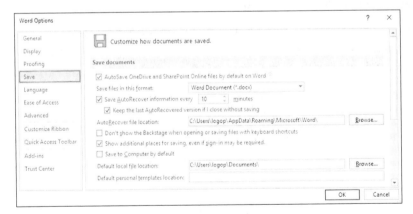

Configure AutoRecover options on the Save page of the Word Options dialog box.

You can change the time interval for saving versions of your documents (the default interval is 10 minutes). You can also change the default AutoRecover file location, moving it from the AppData folder in your user profile to a folder that's more easily accessible, for example. By default, Word also retains the last version that it saved automatically if you close a document without saving it. (These settings apply only to Word and not to other Office programs.)

You can manage and recover versions of documents on the Info page of the Backstage view. Versions of the file that were saved automatically are listed under Manage Document. Right-clicking an item in the list displays options that you can use to open that version, delete the version, or compare that version with the current one.

When you open an autosaved version, Word displays a message bar telling you that the version is a recovered file that is temporarily stored on your computer. On the message bar, you can click Compare to view the differences between the version you opened and the last saved version. Clicking Restore overwrites the last saved version with the version of the document you opened.

You can also recover an unsaved version of a document from the Info page. Clicking the Recover Unsaved Documents option displays the Open dialog box and shows the contents of the Unsaved Files folder, which is part of the AppData folder structure in your user profile. When you open a file from the Unsaved Files folder, Word displays the Save As button on the message bar.

To restore an autosaved version of a document

1. With the document open, click the **File** tab.

2. On the **Info** page, under **Manage Document**, right-click an autosaved version of the file, then click **Open Version**.

3. In the message bar, click **Restore**, then click **OK** to confirm the operation.

To recover an unsaved version of a document

1. On the **Info** page for the document, click **Manage Document**, then click **Recover Unsaved Documents**.

2. In the **Open** dialog box, select the file, then click **Open**.

3. On the message bar, click **Save As**, and in the **Save As** dialog box, name and save the file.

Compare and combine documents

When you work with other authors and reviewers on multiple copies of the same document, you can collect the copies and then use the Combine command to merge the documents and produce a single document that displays and identifies revisions.

Other times you might simply want to compare two versions of a document to view how the versions differ. In this instance, you aren't concerned about who made revisions; you just want to know how the content in one version compares with the content in the other.

The Compare and Combine commands on the Review tab provide similar results when you merge documents, but you apply these commands in different circumstances. Use Compare when you want to view the differences between two versions of a document. Use the Combine command to merge revisions made in multiple copies of a document and to identify who made the revisions.

When you compare two versions of a document, the differences between the original document and the revised document are shown in the original document (or in a new document) as tracked changes. To get the best results when you use the Compare command, make sure that the original and the revised documents do not contain any tracked changes. If either document does, Word treats the changes as accepted when it compares the documents.

In the Compare Documents dialog box, you select the original document and the revised document. Clicking the More button to expand the dialog box enables you to choose settings for the types of changes Word will mark and to specify whether Word shows the results of the comparison in the original document, the revised document, or a new document.

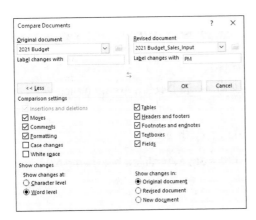

Clear check boxes of elements that you don't want to compare.

By default, all the options in the Comparison Settings area are selected. You can clear the check box for any option other than Insertions And Deletions. If you don't need to view formatting differences, for example, clear the Formatting option. If you are interested chiefly in comparing the differences in the main body of each document, you might also clear the check boxes for Comments, Case Changes (whether a character is lowercase or uppercase), White Space, Headers And Footers, and Fields. In the Show Changes area, Word Level is selected by default. Select the Character Level option if you want Word to mark when a change is made to a few characters of a word, such as when only the case of the first letter is changed. At the Word level, the entire word is shown as a revision when the documents are compared; at the Character level, only the letter is shown as a revision.

In the Show Changes In area, you can select Original Document to display the differences in that document (although you might not want to alter the original document in that way). Or you can select Revised Document to add changes to that document or New Document to create a document based on the original, with the differences made in the revised document shown with tracked changes.

The differences that are shown in the document created by a comparison are attributed to a single author. You can use the Previous and Next buttons in the Changes group on the Review tab to move from change to change, view the changes, and accept or reject the differences.

Exam Strategy The objective domain for Exam MO-101, "Microsoft Word Expert (Word and Word 2019)," requires you to demonstrate the ability to navigate changes in the comparison document. You will not be required to manage tracked changes in any other way.

You can also view the compared, original, and revised document at the same time (if that isn't the view Word provides when it completes the comparison) by clicking Show Source Documents on the Compare menu and then clicking Show Both. Other options on the Show Source Documents menu include Hide Source Documents (which removes the original and the revised document from the view, keeping the compared document), Show Original, and Show Revised.

The Combine Documents dialog box is set up in essentially the same way as the Compare Documents dialog box. When you combine documents, differences between the original and revised documents are shown as tracked changes. If a revised document includes tracked changes, these changes are also displayed in the combined document as tracked changes. Each reviewer is also identified in the combined document.

When you click OK in the Combine Documents dialog box, Word is likely to display a message box telling you that only one set of formatting changes can be stored in the merged document. You need to choose between the changes in the original document or the revised document to continue merging the documents. Word displays the results of combining the documents in a set of windows that shows the combined document in a central pane and the original and revised documents in smaller panes at the right.

Word also displays the Revisions pane along the left side of the window.

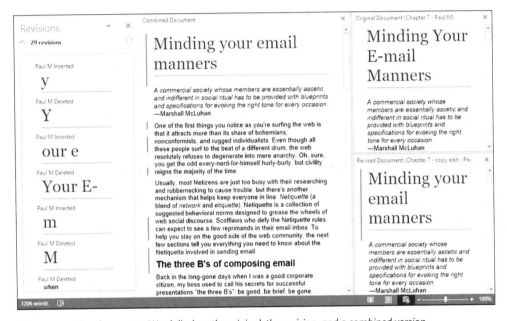

When comparing documents, Word displays the original, the revision, and a combined version.

Tip In the window that Word displays after you combine documents, you can scroll through the combined document and the original and revised documents at the same time. Your location in each document is synchronized, so you can refer to any of the documents as you need to.

You can combine another copy of the document with the merged document by choosing Combine from the Compare menu again, selecting the combined result document as the original document, and selecting the next file you want to merge.

After you save and name the combined document, you can open that document and work through the variations (indicated by tracked changes), accepting and rejecting them to achieve a final document.

To compare documents

1. Do any of the following:

   - Open a blank document.
   - Open the original document.
   - Open the revised document.

2. On the **Review** tab, in the **Compare** group, click **Compare**, then click **Compare** on the menu.

3. In the **Compare Documents** dialog box, select the original document (if it isn't already selected) from the list or by clicking the folder icon and browsing to the location where the document is saved.

4. Select the revised document you want to compare with the original document.

5. In the **Label changes with** box for the revised document, specify the username or initials you want to attribute differences to.

6. If the **Comparison settings** area is not displayed, click **More**.

7. In the **Comparison settings** area, clear or select the check boxes to specify the document elements you want Word to use in its comparison.

8. In the **Show changes at** area, choose whether to show changes at the character level or at the word level.

9. In the **Show changes in** area, choose where you want Word to show changes: in the original document, in the revised document, or in a new document.

10. Click **OK**. If Word prompts you about tracked changes, click **Yes** to complete the comparison.

To combine two or more documents

1. Open a blank document in Word. (You can also start with the original document or one of the revised documents open.)

2. On the **Review** tab, in the **Compare** group, click **Compare**, then click **Combine**.

3. In the **Combine Documents** dialog box, select the original document (if it isn't already selected) from the list or by clicking the folder icon and browsing to the location where the document is saved.

4. Select the revised document you want to combine with the original document.

5. In the **Label changes with** box for the original and revised document, specify the username or initials you want to attribute differences to.

6. If the **Comparison settings** area is not displayed, click **More**.

7. In the **Comparison settings** area, clear or select the check boxes to specify the document elements you want Word to use in its comparison.

8. In the **Show changes at** area, choose whether to show changes at the character level or at the word level.

9. In the **Show changes in** area, choose where you want Word to show changes: in the original document, in the revised document, or in a new document.

10. Click **OK**.

11. In the message box, specify whether to use formatting in the original document or the revised document.

12. Click **Continue with Merge**.

Link to external document content

The tasks involved in managing documents can encompass not only working with multiple Word documents but also working with external data or files that you link to from a Word document. You can link to the content in another Word document and to files created in other Office programs or to Adobe Acrobat documents, for example. You can link to the content of the source file, embed the contents of a file, or display the file as an icon. You can also create an object (such as a chart or a slide) to insert in a Word document.

To link to external data, you use either the Object dialog box or the Insert File dialog box. In the Object dialog box, you can create an object by selecting the object type from a list. You can display the object as an icon instead of the full object; then, in the Word document, you can double-click the icon to open the object. By default, Word embeds the content of the file you select in the document. If you select Link To File, Word creates a link to the source file so that updates to the source file are reflected in the Word document. When you link to a file, Word displays an image of the file in the Word document. Double-clicking this image opens the source program.

In the Insert File dialog box, you can select a file to include in the current document. When you select the Insert As Link command to link to the file, Word inserts a field code by using the INCLUDETEXT field. This field creates a dynamic link to the source file so that updates to that file are reflected in the document in which you created the link. Be mindful that the INCLUDETEXT field uses the full path to the file you insert. If you move or rename the file you have linked to and then update the field, Word displays an error message indicating that the field refers to an invalid file name.

To link to external data

1. On the **Insert** tab, in the **Text** group, click **Object**.

2. In the **Object** dialog box, click the **Create from File** tab.

3. In the **File name** box, enter the name of the file you want to link to, or click **Browse** and then navigate to and select the file.

4. In the **Object** dialog box, select the **Link to file** check box, then click **OK**.

To link to a file

1. On the **Insert** tab, in the **Text** group, open the **Object** menu, then click **Text from File**.

2. In the **Insert File** dialog box, click the file you want to insert.

3. Click the **Insert** arrow, then click **Insert as Link**.

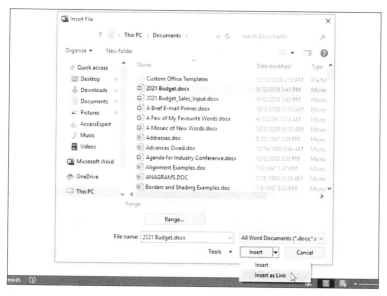

Choose Insert As Link to add a field to a document, linking to the content in the source file.

Customize the Quick Access toolbar

The Quick Access Toolbar offers one-click access to common commands such as Save and Undo. By default, the Quick Access Toolbar appears above the ribbon. This spot is good if you have only a few commands on the Quick Access Toolbar because the relatively small size of the Quick Access Toolbar means that Word has enough room to display the document title and application name. If you want to load up the Quick Access Toolbar with several commands, consider moving it below the ribbon. Doing so gives the Quick Access Toolbar the full width of the window, although it does reduce slightly the amount of vertical space available for your document content. To regain that vertical space (and then some), you can collapse the ribbon.

To get the most out of the Quick Access Toolbar, populate it with the commands you use most often. Note that you are not restricted to just a few commands. If you place the Quick Access Toolbar below the ribbon, you can use the full width of the window, plus you get a More Controls icon at the end of the toolbar that enables you to display a whole other row of commands.

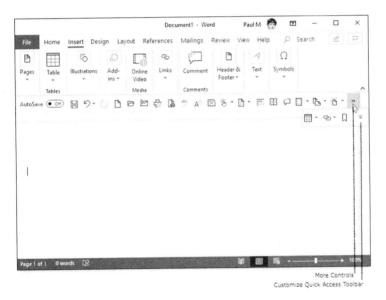

You can display the Quick Access Toolbar below the ribbon.

To change the position of the Quick Access toolbar

1. Click **Customize Quick Access Toolbar**.

2. Click **Show Below the Ribbon**.

To customize the Quick Access toolbar commands

→ If the command you want to add is on the ribbon, right-click the command, then click **Add to Quick Access Toolbar**.

Or,

1. Click **Customize Quick Access Toolbar**.

2. Click **More Commands**.

3. In the **Word Options** dialog box, on the **Quick Access Toolbar** page, use the **Choose Commands From** list to select the command category you want to use.

4. Click the command you want to add.

5. Click **Add**.

6. To change the command position within the Quick Access Toolbar, click the command, then click **Move Up** or **Move Down**.

7. Click **OK**.

Tip If you no longer need a command on the Quick Access Toolbar, right-click the command and then click Remove From Quick Access Toolbar.

Display hidden ribbon tabs

The tabs that Word displays on the ribbon change when you work in different contexts and with different elements of a document. For example, when you select a table, Word displays the Table Tools tabs—Design and Layout. These are known as *contextual tabs*, since they are hidden until Word's context changes (for example, you click a table to select it).

However, don't confuse tabs that are hidden when they are out of context with those tabs that Word hides by default (that is, no matter what the context). You can change which tabs are displayed on the ribbon yourself by choosing settings in the Word Options dialog box. Among the options are whether tabs that are hidden by default are displayed. The Developer tab is an example of a hidden tab that you can choose to display.

∞∞∞

Exam Strategy The objective domain for Exam MO-101, "Microsoft Word Expert (Word and Word 2019)," requires you to demonstrate the ability to display hidden ribbon tabs. You will not be required to customize the ribbon in any other way.

∞∞∞

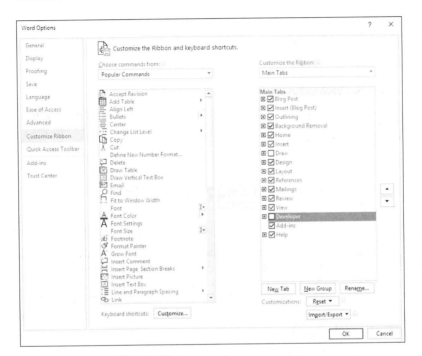

The Developer tab is hidden by default.

To display hidden ribbon tabs

1. On the **File** tab, click **Options**.

2. In the **Word Options** dialog box, click **Customize Ribbon**.

   Tip You can display the Customize Ribbon page of the Word Options dialog box directly by right-clicking anywhere within the ribbon or the Quick Access Toolbar and then clicking Customize The Ribbon.

   ---

3. On the **Customize Ribbon** page, in the **Customize the Ribbon** list, select the check box for the tab you want to display. For example, select the **Developer** check box to display the **Developer** tab.

4. Click **OK** to apply your settings.

Change the Normal template default font

When you set a default font, documents you create use that font and the settings you defined for it (font size, font color, and so on). In Word documents based on the Normal template, the default font is used in the definition of the Normal style and for styles based on the Normal style. The default font is also associated with the body font that is defined for the currently applied theme. You can change the Normal template default font by specifying settings in the Font dialog box and then clicking the Set As Default button.

See Also For information about building custom theme fonts, see "Create custom font sets" in "Objective 3.2: Create custom design elements."

To change the default font

1. Create or open a document that is based on Word's Normal template.

2. On the **Home** tab, in the **Font** group, click the dialog box launcher.

3. On the **Font** tab of the **Font** dialog box, select the options that you want to use for the default font.

4. Click **Set As Default**.

5. In the message box that appears, select **All Documents Based On the Normal Template**.

6. Click **OK**.

Objective 1.1 practice tasks

The practice files for these tasks are located in the **MOSWordExpert2019\Objective1** practice file folder. The folder also contains result files that you can use to check your work.

➤ Start Word and do the following:

- ❑ Use the Combine command to merge the **WordExpert_1-1a** (original) and **WordExpert_1-1b** (revised) documents, using the default settings and merging formatting from the **WordExpert_1-1b** document.

- ❑ Save the document in the practice file folder as *WordExpert_1-1_combined*.

- ❑ Open the **WordExpert_1-1a_results** document. Compare this document with **WordExpert_1-1_combined** to check your work. Then close the **WordExpert_1-1a_results** document.

- ❑ Open the **WordExpert_1-1c** document, and then insert the text of the **WordExpert_1-1c** document into the **WordExpert_1-1_combined** document after the title.

- ❑ Open the **WordExpert_1-1c_results** document. Compare the two documents to check your work.

- ❑ Close all open documents.

Objective 1.2: Prepare documents for collaboration

Preparing a document for collaboration with other users can involve several steps. You might need to restrict the editing of a document so that reviewers can only enter comments, for example, and not make changes directly to the text. You can also specify sections of a document that can be edited only by certain individuals.

Word also provides options to protect a document with a password and to mark a document as final, which notifies users who open the document that the document is considered complete.

This topic guides you in studying the steps involved in preparing documents for collaboration.

When you share a document to obtain comments from peers or colleagues or for someone to make revisions to sections of the document, you don't want reviewers to modify the document at will by changing the formatting, adding or deleting content, inserting graphics, or making other modifications. Documents that contain important data or that you plan to use as the focus of a report or presentation can be protected before you share them. You can use options available in Word to restrict the types of changes users can make to a document, specify who can edit a document, and mark which sections of a document specific individuals can edit.

To control how a document can be edited, you set options in the Restrict Editing pane.

Use the settings in the Restrict Editing pane to allow specific people to edit all or part of the document.

The pane has three sections:

- **Formatting restrictions** Select the check box in this area to limit formatting to a specific set of styles and to prevent users of a document from modifying styles and applying local formatting. From the Restrict Editing pane, you can open the Formatting Restrictions dialog box, where you can select the styles that are available to users working with the document. You can allow all styles, allow only a minimum set of styles recommended by Word, specify that no styles can be applied, or select the specific styles you want to use. The options at the bottom of the Formatting Restrictions dialog box control whether users can switch themes or substitute quick styles and whether settings for automatic formatting can override the restrictions you specify.

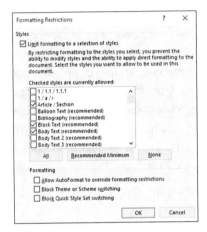

Select the styles and formatting options you want to allow in a document.

- **Editing restrictions** Use the Editing Restrictions area to control the types of changes users can make to the document. Word offers the following four settings:

  - **No changes (Read only)** This prevents users from making revisions, although you can set up exceptions that allow specific users to edit all or certain sections of the document.

  - **Tracked changes** Revisions made to the document are indicated by revision marks. Tracked changes cannot be turned off without removing protection from the document; removing protection can be controlled by defining a password.

- **Comments** Users can add comments to the document, but they can't make revisions to the document's content itself. For this option, you can set up exceptions for specific users.

- **Filling in forms** This option lets you restrict input to filling in form controls (such as check boxes and list boxes) that are part of a document.

■ **Start Enforcement** After you define the formatting and editing restrictions you want to apply to the document, use the Start Enforcing Protection dialog box to define a password that's required to remove protection from the document.

If you select No Changes (Read Only) or Comments, you can use the Exceptions area to specify users who can edit the whole document or sections of it. Exceptions apply to the complete document by default, but you can apply exceptions to a particular section of a document by selecting that section and then designating the people who can edit it. You can also allow everyone to edit specific sections, and you can apply different exceptions to different sections of a document. Clicking the More Users link opens the Add Users dialog box, where you can specify the names of people who are granted an exception.

IMPORTANT The More Users link in the Exceptions area works only if you are part of a network domain. If you are part of a domain, you can use More Users to add users who are also part of the same domain. If you are not on a domain, you won't be able to add exceptions for individual users.

If you specify editing exceptions, you and other users can locate and display the sections of a document that a specific user can edit by selecting the check box beside a user's name in the Restrict Editing pane.

As a step in completing a document you have worked on with a group, you can mark the document as final so that colleagues or coworkers know the document's status. Marking a document as final provides a notification of its status; it does not prevent users from making changes (users can turn off the feature), and it does not provide the same level of protection as applying a password to the document.

When a user opens a document that is marked final, Word displays the message bar, notifying the user of the document's status. In addition, the title bar of the document window indicates that the file's status is read-only.

For a document marked as final, the user must intentionally activate the document to make changes.

When you save a document from the Save As dialog box, you can display the General Options dialog box and then define a password that users need to enter to open the document, in addition to a password that's required to modify the document.

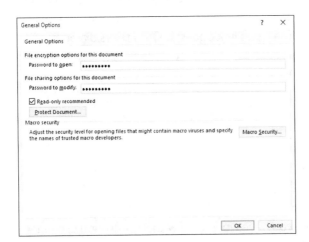

The General Options dialog box is available only from the Save As dialog box.

IMPORTANT Be careful to retain the passwords you assign. Word provides no way for you to recover these passwords.

Keep in mind that requiring users to enter a password before they modify a document is intended to protect a document from unintentional editing. Defining this password does not encrypt a document to help secure it from malicious users.

Tip Encryption enhances the security of a document by scrambling the contents so that it can be read only by someone who has a password or another type of key.

To protect a document through encryption, you can use the Protect Document command on the Info page of the Backstage view. When you define an encryption password, Word cautions you that the password cannot be recovered.

To restrict editing and formatting

1. On the **Review** tab, click **Restrict Editing**.

   Tip Alternatively, click File, click the Info page, click Protect Document, and then click Restrict Editing.

2. In the **Restrict Editing** pane, select the options you want to apply:

   - To specify a set of styles users can apply, select the **Limit formatting to a selection of styles** check box, then click **Settings**. In the **Formatting Restrictions** dialog box, select the set of styles and formatting options you want to make available in the document, then click **OK**.

   - To control the type of editing allowed in the document, select the **Allow only this type of editing in the document** check box, then choose from the options in the list. Define exceptions by selecting a section of the document and then choosing which users can edit the selected section.

3. Click **Yes, Start Enforcing Protection**.

4. In the **Start Enforcing Protection** dialog box, if you want to prevent other readers from removing the protection without permission, enter and reenter a password. Then click **OK**.

To mark a document as final

1. On the **Info** page of the Backstage view, click **Protect Document**, then click **Mark as Final**.

2. Click **OK** to confirm the operation and save the document.

Tip Word might display a message box describing the effects of marking a document as final. Select the Do Not Show Again check box if you no longer need Word to display this message, then click OK.

To define passwords required to open or modify a document

1. Click **File**, click either **Save As** (for a local file) or **Save a Copy** (for a OneDrive file), and then click **More Options**.

2. In the **Save As** dialog box, click **Tools**, then click **General Options**.

3. In the **General Options** dialog box, do either or both of the following:

    - In the **Password to open** box, enter a password for opening the document.

    - In the **Password to modify** box, enter a password for making modifications.

4. In the **General Options** dialog box, click **OK**.

5. In each **Confirm Password** dialog box that opens, reenter the appropriate password.

6. In the **Save As** dialog box, click **Save**.

To encrypt a file with a password

1. On the **Info** page of the Backstage view, click **Protect Document**, and then click **Encrypt with Password**.

2. In the **Encrypt Document** dialog box, enter the password you want to use, then click **OK**.

3. In the **Confirm Password** dialog box, reenter the password, then click **OK**.

To remove password protection

1. Open the **General Options** dialog box or the **Encrypt Document** dialog box.

2. Delete the password that you want to remove, then click **OK**.

Objective 1.2 practice tasks

The practice file for these tasks is located in the **MOSWordExpert2019\ Objective1** practice file folder. The folder also contains a result file that you can use to check your work.

➤ Open the **WordExpert_1-2** document, and do the following:

❑ Display the Restrict Editing pane.

❑ Configure the editing restrictions to permit only comments and no other changes.

❑ Set up an exception that allows users to edit the Preface section of the document.

❑ Start enforcing protection and assign the password **WordExpert** to enforce protection (and to turn off protection when necessary).

❑ Encrypt the document content by assigning the password **WordExpert** to the document.

❑ Mark the document as final.

➤ Save the document.

➤ Open the **WordExpert_1-2_results** document, using the password *WordExpert*. Compare the two documents to check your work. Then close the documents.

Objective 1.3: Use and configure language options

Word offers a number of options for working in different languages. For example, you can add new authoring languages and you can configure other languages for the ribbon, buttons, and other display features. With extra languages installed, you can add and edit text in another language, proof in another language, and translate sections of text and entire documents. This section takes you through Word's options for configuring and using other languages.

Configure authoring and display languages

You can change the language that Word uses for authoring and for the display (the ribbon, buttons, tabs, and other interface features). You are free to apply a different language for authoring and display, depending on the languages available in the version of Windows or Office that you are using and the Windows language packs that you have installed. You can install additional languages from the Language page of the Word Options dialog box. If you have multiple languages installed, you can tell Word which language you prefer to use. You can also set a language priority order, which tells Word which languages to use, in order, if the display language is not available in your default language.

To add an authoring language

1. Click **File**, click **Options**.

2. In the **Word Options** dialog box, on the **Language** page, click **Add a Language**.

3. Use the **Add an Authoring Language** list to select the language you want to install.

4. Click **Add**. Word adds the language to the **Office Authoring Languages and Proofing** list.

Tip For your new language, if you see Proofing Available, then you need to install the associated language pack from the Office.com website. Click the Proofing Available link to display the language pack page, click Download, and then run the downloaded file to install the language pack.

When you add a language, Word displays it in the Office Authoring Languages And Proofing list.

To change the display language priority order

→ In the **Word Options** dialog box, on the **Language** page, click a language in the **Office Display Language** list, then use the **Move Up** (higher priority) and **Move Down** (lower priority) buttons to position the language in the list.

Tip To add more display languages, click the Install Additional Display Languages From Office.com link, which opens a page that enables you to download a language pack accessory for Office.

Use the Move Up and Move Down buttons to set a language's priority.

To set the preferred languages

→ In the **Word Options** dialog box, on the **Language** page, click a language in the **Office Authoring Languages and Proofing** list, then click the **Set Preferred** button that appears to the right of the list.

→ In the **Word Options** dialog box, on the **Language** page, click a language in the **Office Display Language** list, then click the **Set Preferred** button that appears the right of the list.

To remove an authoring language

→ In the **Word Options** dialog box, on the **Language** page, click a language in the **Office Authoring Languages and Proofing** list, click **Remove**, and then restart Word to put the change into effect.

Use language-specific features

With your languages configured, you can now switch from one language to another within Word. For example, you can switch to another language to add or edit Word data and you can set another language as Word's default proofing dictionary.

Another language tool that comes in handy when you are working with other languages is the Translate command on the Review tab. This command opens the Translator task pane, which includes From and To boxes, where From shows the original text and To shows the language to which you want the original text translated. Translator attempts to recognize the original language, but if it gets the language wrong, you can select the correct language from a list. You can also select the language to which you want the original text translated.

To add and edit text in another language

→ In the **Word Options** dialog box, on the **Language** page, click a language in the **Office Authoring Languages and Proofing** list, then click the **Set Preferred** button that appears to the right of the list.

To proof in another language

1. Click **File**, then click **Options**.

2. In the **Word Options** dialog box, on the **Proofing** page, click **Custom Dictionaries**.

3. Use the **Dictionary Language** list to select the language you want to use, then click **OK**.

Use the Dictionary Language list to select a proofing language.

To translate a selection of text

1. Select the text you want to translate.

2. On the **Review** tab, in the **Language** group, click **Translate**, then click **Translate Selection**. The **Translator** pane appears.

Use the Translator pane to translate text from one language to another.

3. If Translator did not select the correct original language, use the **From** list to select the language.

4. Use the **To** list to select the language to which you want the original text translated.

To translate an entire document

1. Open the document you want to translate.

2. On the **Review** tab, in the **Language** group, click **Translate**, then click **Translate Document**. The **Translator** pane appears.

The Translator pane for the translation of an entire document.

3. If Translator did not select the correct original language, use the **From** list to select the language. If you are not sure which language to use, select **Auto-Detect** instead.

4. Use the **To** list to select the language to which you want the original text translated.

5. Click **Translate**. Word creates a new document for the translated text.

Objective 1.3 practice tasks

The practice file for these tasks is located in the **MOSWordExpert2019\
Objective1** practice file folder.

➤ Open the **WordExpert_1-3** document and do the following:

❏ Add the authoring language French (Canada).

❏ Add the language French as a display language.

❏ In the Office Display Language list, select French, and move its
priority up and then down.

❏ In the Office Authoring Languages and Proofing list, select French
(Canada), set it as the preferred language, and then return the
preferred language to the original.

❏ In the Office Authoring Languages and Proofing list, select
French (Canada), remove it, restart Word, and then reopen the
WordExpert_1-3 workbook.

❏ Select the document title, and run the Translate Selection command
to translate the French text into English.

Objective group 2

Use advanced editing and formatting features

The skills tested in this section of the Microsoft Office Specialist Expert exam for Microsoft Word 365 and Microsoft Word 2019 relate to using Word's advanced editing and formatting features. Specifically, the following objectives are associated with this set of skills:

2.1 Perform advanced editing and formatting

2.2 Configure paragraph layout options

2.3 Create and manage styles

This chapter guides you in studying the ways in which you can edit and format long, complex documents, such as books, dissertations, reports, and requests for proposals. To begin, this chapter explains some of the advanced editing and formatting features in Word, including how to use wildcards or special characters to search for patterns in text, how to find and replace styles and formatting, and how to work with Word's options for pasting content. In this chapter you also learn how to wield advanced paragraph layout tools such as hyphenation, line numbers, and pagination options. This chapter also describes how to create and modify styles so that you can more easily format a long document and keep the document's appearance consistent.

To complete the practice tasks in this chapter, you need the practice files contained in the **MOSWordExpert2019\Objective2** practice file folder. For more information, see "Download the practice files" in this book's Introduction.

Objective 2.1: Perform advanced editing and formatting

This topic explains how to work with advanced editing and formatting features. It describes how to extend find-and-replace operations by using wildcard characters and how to use special characters when you search for and replace text. It next describes how you can carry out find-and-replace operations by using styles or specific formatting. Finally, this topic also covers Word's options for pasting cut or copied content.

Find and replace text by using wildcards and special characters

Simple find-and-replace operations in Word can be extended in several ways. For example, in the Find And Replace dialog box, you can select an option to search only for whole words, use a case-specific search (*they're* instead of *They're*), or search by using how words sound (*they're*, *their*, and *there*). This section describes another way to extend find-and-replace operations—by using wildcard characters and special characters.

See Also For more information about finding and replacing formatting and styles, see "Find and replace formatting and styles" later in this topic.

Use wildcard characters to find and replace text

You can extend your use of the Find And Replace dialog box by using wildcards. For example, as a wildcard character, the asterisk (*) represents a sequence of one or more characters. The question mark (?) is used to represent a single character within a sequence. When you combine wildcard characters with literal characters, you can find patterns of text.

The following table lists wildcard characters and examples of how to use them.

Wildcard character	Syntax and examples
?	Locates any single character. For example, *l?w* locates the words *law* and *low* and this sequence of characters in words such as *below* or *lawful*.
*	Locates a string of characters. For example, *J*n* finds *John*, *Jocelyn*, and *Johnson*. Wildcard character sequences are case-sensitive. To find *joinery* and *journey*, you would use *j*n*.

Wildcard character	Syntax and examples
<	Finds characters at the start of a word. For example, *<plen* finds *plenty*, *plentiful*, and *plentitude*. It does not find the word *splendid*.
>	Finds characters at the end of a word. For example, *ful>* finds *fanciful*, *useful*, and *plentiful*. It does not find *fulfill* or *wonderfully*.
[ ]	Finds one of the characters within a sequence you specify. For example, *h[eor]s* finds words such as *ghosts*, *these*, *hose*, *those*, and *searches*, or the abbreviation *hrs* (hours). It does not find *horse*.
[n-n]	Finds any single character within the range you specify. You must specify the range in ascending order (*d-l*, for example). For instance, *[c-h]ave* finds *gave*, *have*, and *leave*.
[!n-n]	Finds any single character except the characters in the range you specify. For example, *st[!n-z]ck* finds *stack* and *stick* but not *stock* or *stuck*.
{n}	Finds the specified number of instances of the previous character or expression. For example, *cre{2}d* finds *creed* (two instances of *e*) but does not find *credential*.
{n,}	Finds at least the specified number of instances of the preceding character or expression. For example, *cre{1,}d* finds both *creed* and *credential*.
{n,m}	Finds the number of instances of the preceding character or expression in a range. For example, *50{1,3}* finds *50*, *500*, and *5000*.
@	Finds one or more instances of the preceding character or expression. For example, *bal@** finds *balloon* and *balcony*.
[\wildcard character]	Finds instances of the specified wildcard character. For example, *[*]* finds all asterisk wildcard characters.

As shown in the example for the @ symbol, you can combine wildcard characters to create expressions. For example, the expression *s[a-n]{2}d* finds words such as *send*, *sending*, *dashed*, and *slide*, but it does not find the word *sad*. In this expression, Word searches for a string of characters that starts with *s*, contains two characters within the range *a-n*, and ends with *d*. You can also use parentheses to group wildcard characters and text to indicate the order of evaluation. For example, the expression *<(det)*(ing)>* finds *determining* and *deterring*, with the character sequence *det* at the start of the word (indicated by the < symbol) and the sequence *ing* at the end (indicated by the > symbol). Keep in mind that all searches in which you use wildcards are case-sensitive. As an example, the expression *[c-h]ave* finds *have* and *cave* but not the name *Dave*.

Tip When the Use Wildcards option is selected in the Find And Replace dialog box, the wildcard characters you can use appear on the Special menu. You can then select a character or enter the character or characters you want to use in the Find What and Replace With boxes.

You can also use wildcards to replace patterns of text. For example, you can use the *\n* wildcard character to invert first and last names by entering *(First Name) (Last Name)* (that is, a person's actual first and last names, each enclosed in parentheses) in the Find What box and **\2 \1** in the Replace With box. Word finds occurrences of the name and inverts the order so that the last name (item **2**) comes first.

To display the Replace tab of the Find And Replace dialog box

→ On the **Home** tab, in the **Editing** group, click **Replace**.

→ Press **Ctrl+H**.

To search and replace by using wildcard characters

1. Display the **Replace** tab of the **Find and Replace** dialog box.

2. If the **Search Options** area isn't displayed, click **More**.

3. Select the **Use wildcards** check box.

4. In the **Find what** box, enter the wildcard expression for the text you want to find. Select wildcard characters from the **Special** menu or enter the wildcard character sequence yourself.

5. In the **Replace with** box, enter any replacement text or select an option from the **Special** menu.

6. Click **Find Next** to locate the first instance of the search term.

7. Click **Replace** or **Replace All** as appropriate to replace the search term.

Use special characters to find and replace text

To find and replace formatting marks, a character such as an em dash, or a field, you make selections from the Special menu in the Find And Replace dialog box. Special characters are represented by a character combination that begins with the caret symbol (^).

Insert character codes from the Special menu to find and replace special characters such as paragraph marks, notes, and dashes.

In a document with extra paragraph characters, for example, you could search for two paragraph characters (^p^p) and replace the pair with one. If you wanted to search for any year between 2000 and 2009 and replace each year with 2019, you could enter **2^#^#^#** (a 2 and three instances of the Any Digit option) in the Find What box and **2019** in the Replace With box.

Items on the Special menu vary depending on whether you are specifying values in the Find What box or the Replace With box. For example, you can choose *Clipboard Contents* as the value in the Replace With box to replace what you are searching for with the content saved on the Clipboard.

To search and replace by using special characters

1. Display the **Replace** tab of the **Find and Replace** dialog box. If necessary, click **More** to display the **Search Options** area.

2. In the **Find what** box, enter any text that you want to include in the search term.

3. Click the **Special** button, then on the menu, click the special character you want to enter in the box. Repeat as necessary to enter multiple special characters.

4. In the **Replace with** box, enter any replacement text or special characters.

5. Click **Find Next** to locate the first instance of the search term.

6. Click **Replace** or **Replace All** as appropriate to replace the search term.

Find and replace formatting and styles

In the Find And Replace dialog box, you can use the Format menu to locate text formatted with a specific font, for example, and then replace that font with another. You can also search for formatting attributes such as font size or color, paragraph settings such as line spacing, specific tab settings, text in a specific language, or text or other document elements to which a specific style is applied.

The options on the Format menu open dialog boxes like those that you open from the Home tab to apply or modify formatting. In those dialog boxes, you select or enter settings for the format you want to search for (for example, 12-point Arial font with italic applied), and then specify settings for the new formatting you want to apply (such as 14-point Calibri with a red font color).

When you select Style on the Format menu, you can use options in the Find Style dialog box to specify a style you want to locate and a style with which you want to replace that style.

In the Description area, you can verify the attributes of the style you're searching for.

When you use these find-and-replace operations to find and replace only formatting or styles (leaving the related text unchanged), you don't enter any text or other values in the Find What and Replace With boxes. However, you can search for and replace text by using the formatting or style applied to that text. For example, you could search for instances of the text *Office 2013* that have the Version Number style applied and replace those instances with the text *Office 2019*.

To find and replace formatting

1. Display the **Replace** tab of the **Find and Replace** dialog box. If necessary, click **More** to display the **Search Options** area.

2. Click in the **Find what** box, then click **Format**. On the **Format** menu, click the type of formatting you want to find. In the dialog box that opens, specify the formatting, then click **OK**.

3. Click in the **Replace with** box. On the **Format** menu, click the command for the type of formatting you need. In the dialog box that opens, specify the formatting you want to substitute, then click **OK**.

4. Click **Find Next** to locate the first instance of the formatting.

5. Click **Replace** or **Replace All** as appropriate to substitute the new formatting.

To find and replace styles

1. Display the **Replace** tab of the **Find and Replace** dialog box. If necessary, click **More** to display the **Search Options** area.

2. Click in the **Find what** box, then click **Format**.

3. On the **Format** menu, click **Style**.

4. In the **Find Style** dialog box, click the style you want to find, then click **OK**.

5. Click in the **Replace with** box.

6. On the **Format** menu, click **Style**.

7. In the **Replace Style** dialog box, click the style you want to substitute, then click **OK**.

8. Click **Find Next** to locate the first instance of the style.

9. Click **Replace** or **Replace All** as appropriate to substitute the new style.

To find and replace text by using formatting or styles

1. Display the **Replace** tab of the **Find and Replace** dialog box. If necessary, click **More** to display the **Search Options** area.

2. Click in the **Find what** box, enter the text you want to find, then click **Format**.

3. On the **Format** menu, click the command for the type of formatting applied to the text or click **Style** to search for text with a specific style applied.

4. In the dialog box that opens, specify the formatting or style, then click **OK**.

5. In the **Replace with** box, enter the text you want to substitute.

6. Click **Find Next** to locate the first instance of the text.

7. Click **Replace** or **Replace All** as appropriate to substitute the new style.

Apply paste options

Pasting cut or copied text and other content is a common editing task that applies when you're working with a single Word document, multiple Word documents, or content from another program. The document (or document location) where the content was cut or copied is called the *source*, and the document where the content is to be pasted is called the *destination*. As a general rule, if the styles in the documents you are working with have the same definitions, the text and other content will retain the formatting from the source. If the same styles in the source and destination have conflicting definitions, Word uses the style definition in the destination by default.

To control how styles get applied during a paste, or to resolve a conflict in styles between the source and destination, you can use the Paste Options button, which Word displays whenever you paste content. You click the button (or press Ctrl) to open a gallery of icons that provides options for how the content you are pasting should be formatted. You can use the destination formatting, use the source formatting, merge formatting, or keep only the text (so that the content is pasted using the default Normal style). If Live Preview is enabled, Word displays how each option affects the display of the pasted content when you point to the option's icon.

Use the Paste Options gallery to specify how you want Word to paste the content.

Depending on the content you paste, the Paste Options gallery includes some or all of the following icons:

- **Use Destination Styles** Click this icon (or press **S** while the gallery is displayed) to paste the content using the styles as defined in the destination document.

- **Picture** (Word 365 only) Click this icon (or press **U** while the gallery is displayed) to paste the content as a picture object (that is, you end up with a noneditable image of the original text, not the text itself).

- **Keep Source Formatting** Click this icon (or press **K** while the gallery is displayed) to paste the content using the styles as defined in the source document.

- **Merge Formatting** Click this icon (or press **M** while the gallery is displayed) to paste the content without any formatting that was applied directly to the content, except for emphasis formatting (such as bold and italic) that has been applied to only portions of the content. The pasted content assumes the styles and formatting that are in effect at the insertion point.

- **Keep Text Only** Click this icon (or press **T** while the gallery is displayed) to discard all the source formatting (as well as any nontext elements such as images) and paste the content so that it assumes the styles and formatting that are in effect at the insertion point.

Tip When you hover the mouse pointer over a Paste Options gallery icon, Word applies a live preview of the paste option to the pasted content, which enables you to see in advance if a particular paste option produces the effect you want.

By selecting settings on the Advanced page of the Word Options dialog box (or clicking Set Default Paste in the Paste Options gallery), you can control Word's default paste option in four pasting scenarios: Pasting Within the Same Document, Pasting Between Documents, Pasting Between Documents When Style Definitions Conflict, and Pasting From Other Programs. You can also specify a default paste behavior for images.

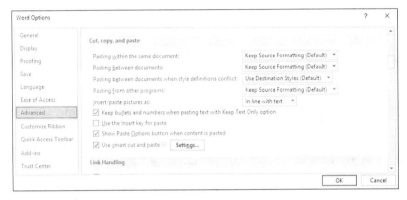

Configure options for pasting content.

In the rest of the Cut, Copy, And Paste section, you can set other default pasting behaviors. For example, by default Word preserves bullets and numbers when you use the Keep Text Only paste option, but you can turn this off by clearing the Keep Bullets And Numbers When Pasting Text With Keep Text Only Option check box. Rather than using the Ctrl+V key combination to paste content, you can press the Insert key if you select the Use The Insert Key For Paste check box. In the unlikely event that you never use the Paste Options button and therefore find it just gets in the way, you can prevent it from appearing by clearing the Show Paste Options button When Content Is Pasted check box. Finally, you can click the Settings button next to the Use Smart Cut And Paste option to open the Settings dialog box. The Smart Style Behavior option in this dialog box also affects how Word manages style conflicts. When this option is selected, styles are handled consistently when the style in the document you are pasting from has the same name as a style in the document you are pasting to. The paste options allow you to choose between keeping the formatting and matching the formatting of the destination document.

To apply a paste option

1. Paste some content where you want it to appear in a Word document.

2. Click the **Paste Options** button (or press **Ctrl**).

3. Point to the paste option icons, refer to the live preview to view how each option affects the content you are pasting, and then click the option you want to apply.

To set paste options

1. Display the **Advanced** page of the **Word Options** dialog box:

   - Click **File**, click **Options**, and then click **Advanced**.

   - After you paste content, click **Paste Options**, then click **Set Default Paste**.

2. In the **Cut, Copy, and Paste** section, use the four **Pasting X** lists to select the default paste options you want to use.

3. Use the **Insert/Paste Pictures As** list to set the default paste behavior for images.

4. Use the check boxes in the rest of the **Cut, Copy, and Paste** section to set Word's other paste options.

5. To customize Word's Smart Cut and Paste feature, click **Settings**.

Objective 2.1 practice tasks

The practice file for these tasks is located in the **MOSWordExpert2019\ Objective2** practice file folder. The folder also contains a result file that you can use to check your work.

➤ Open the **WordExpert_2-1** document, and do the following:

    ❑ Use wildcards in the Find And Replace dialog box to locate words that start with *calor*.

    ❑ Use the \n wildcard character to replace the phrase *aisle cookie* with **cookie aisle**.

    ❑ Find instances of two consecutive paragraph marks and replace them with a single paragraph mark.

    ❑ Find the instance of the Subtitle style and replace it with the Quote style.

    ❑ Find all the bold text and change the font color to Dark Blue.

➤ Open the **WordExpert_2-1_results** document. Compare the two documents to check your work. Then close the open documents.

Objective 2.2: Configure paragraph layout options

This topic describes Word's advanced paragraph layout options, including how to control hyphenation and add line numbers. Later in this section you also learn how to set paragraph pagination options.

Exam Strategy The objective domain for Exam MO-101, "Microsoft Word Expert (Word and Word 2019)," requires you to demonstrate the ability to lay out a paragraph. You will not be required to work with layout options for larger document objects such as sections and pages.

Configure hyphenation and line numbers

A raging debate among desktop publishers is going on even as you read this: should you justify text—that is, align the text on both the left and right margins—or should you justify only the left margin and leave the right margin ragged? The answer is, "It depends." Many people perceive justified text as a formal look and, therefore, more desirable for formal documents. Others insist that the drawbacks of right justification outweigh the perhaps more casual approach of a ragged-right margin. White space comes into play here, both as a positive and a negative.

When you justify text (that is, align the text on both the left and right margins), Word forces extra spaces between words to make the right margin even. These extra spaces can cause "rivers" of unwanted white space to run through your text. When you justify text in columns, Word has fewer words to work with and might insert whole blocks of spaces to even out the margin. Readers find these blocks extremely distracting. On the other hand, ragged-right margins created by aligning text on the left don't force extra spaces into text and therefore don't cause white space rivers and blank areas. Extra white space at the right margin also helps open up your text, but sometimes your right edges can look too ragged, particularly if you use many long words.

You can solve both problems using Word's hyphenation feature, which hyphenates longer words rather than wrapping them onto the next line:

- In justified text, this means you get more text on each line, so you are less likely to have rivers of white space and blank areas are filled in with partial words.

- In right-ragged text, Word fills in the right edge of each line with either entire words, if they fit, or with partial words as part of the hyphenation process, so the raggedness of the right margin is greatly reduced.

Set your hyphenation options.

Unfortunately, if you hyphenate to reduce raggedness, you run the risk of having hyphens ending too many lines, which is another visual distraction for the reader. If you choose to have Word hyphenate a document automatically, you can set an option to limit the number of consecutive hyphens. If you hyphenate a document manually, Word displays a dialog box in which you can confirm the hyphenation Word suggests or reposition a hyphen within a word.

Tip If you have a paragraph that you do not want hyphenated, you can tell Word to skip it. Right-click anywhere inside the paragraph, then click Paragraph. On the Line And Page Breaks tab, select the Don't Hyphenate check box.

You can specify hyphenation breaks that meet your requirements.

Some documents require the lines to be numbered so that the reader (or writer) can more easily reference a particular line. Legal documents most often require line numbers, but they are also useful for programming code and literary analysis. You can also apply line numbers by section, so you can add them to some or all of a document. Word's Line Numbers command inserts line numbers along the left margin of a document. You can also set line-numbering options such as the distance between line numbers and text.

Tip If you have a paragraph that you do not want to display line numbers, you can tell Word to suppress them. Right-click anywhere inside the paragraph, then click Paragraph. On the Line And Page Breaks tab, select the Suppress Line Numbers check box.

You can display line numbers that use a specific interval by changing the value in the Count By list.

To automatically hyphenate a document

1. On the **Layout** tab, in the **Page Setup** group, click **Hyphenation**, then click **Hyphenation Options**.

2. In the **Hyphenation** dialog box, select the **Automatically hyphenate document** check box.

3. In the **Limit consecutive hyphens to** box, enter or select the maximum number of consecutive hyphenated lines that a paragraph can contain.

4. Click **OK**.

To manually hyphenate a word

1. In the document, select the word you want to hyphenate.

2. On the **Layout** tab, in the **Page Setup** group, click **Hyphenation**, then click **Manual**.

3. In the **Manual Hyphenation** dialog box, accept the hyphenation suggested by Word or insert a hyphen where you want to break the word.

To assign line numbers

→ Select the paragraph or paragraphs you want to work with. On the **Layout** tab, in the **Page Setup** group, click **Line Numbers**, then click a preset option: **None, Continuous, Restart Each Page, Restart Each Section**, or **Suppress for Current Paragraph**.

Or

1. Select the paragraph or paragraphs you want to work with.

2. On the **Layout** tab, in the **Page Setup** group, click **Line Numbers**, then click **Line Numbering Options**.

3. On the **Layout** tab of the **Page Setup** dialog box, click the **Line Numbers** button.

4. In the **Line Numbers** dialog box, select the **Add line numbering** check box.

5. In the **Start at** list, click the beginning line number.

6. In the **From text** list, specify the distance the line number will appear from the left margin of the text, or keep the default setting of **Auto**.

7. In the **Count by** list, specify the increment by which line numbers are displayed.

8. In the **Numbering** area, select the option for how line numbers should be displayed: **Restart each page**, **Restart each section**, or **Continuous**.

9. Click **OK** in the **Line Numbers** dialog box, then click **OK** in the **Page Setup** dialog box.

Set paragraph pagination options

The Line And Page Breaks tab of the Paragraph dialog box provides options that you can use to control various aspects of page layout.

Select one or more of the Pagination options to control how text breaks across a page.

In the Pagination group, use the following settings to manage pagination:

- **Widow/Orphan control** A *widow* is a single line of text that appears at the bottom of a page, and an *orphan* is a single line that appears at the top of a page. Selecting this option controls widows and orphans by preventing single lines of text at either the start or the end of a page.

- **Keep with next** This option keeps the lines of text you select together with the paragraph that follows them. You might apply this setting to a heading and the paragraph that follows it so that the heading does not stand alone on the page.

- **Keep lines together** When you want to keep lines of text together on a page (the stanza of a poem or a quotation, for example), select that text, then set this option.

- **Page break before** Select this option to insert a page break before selected text.

In the Formatting Exceptions area of the Line And Page Breaks tab, there are two options:

- **Suppress line numbers** Use this option to turn off the display of line numbers for the active paragraph.

- **Don't hyphenate** Use this option to turn off hyphenation in the active paragraph.

The Textbox Options area of the dialog box provides settings for controlling whether the text that wraps a text box is tightly wrapped. You can apply one of the following settings to the active paragraph: None, All, First And Last Lines, First Line Only, and Last Line Only.

To set paragraph pagination options

1. Select the paragraph or paragraphs you want to work with.

2. Either right-click the selection and then click **Paragraph** or, on the **Layout** tab, in the **Paragraph** group, click the dialog box launcher.

3. On the **Line and Page Breaks** tab of the **Paragraph** dialog box, do any of the following:

   - In the **Pagination** area, select any of the **Widow/Orphan control**, **Keep with next**, **Keep lines together**, and **Page break before** check boxes.

   - In the **Formatting exceptions** area, select either or both of the **Suppress line numbers** and **Don't hyphenate** check boxes.

   - In the **Textbox options** area, if the **Tight wrap** list is active, select an option for how to wrap text around the selected text box.

4. Click **OK** to apply the settings.

Objective 2.2 practice tasks

The practice file for these tasks is located in the **MOSWordExpert2019\
Objective2** practice file folder. The folder also contains a result file that you
can use to check your work.

➤ Open the **WordExpert_2-2** document, and do the following:

❑ Configure the VBA code listing so that it does not get hyphenated.

❑ Configure the rest of the document (that is, the non-code text) to
suppress line numbers.

❑ Manually hyphenate the entire document, accepting Word's default
hyphen placements (for example, in the first paragraph, the words
sentence and *sentences* should be hyphenated as *sen-tence* and
sen-tences, respectively). However, if Word tries to insert a hyphen
into a code word (that is, any text in a monospace font), decline
the hyphen.

❑ Add continuous line numbers to the VBA code listing.

➤ Open the **WordExpert_2-2_results** document. Compare the two
documents to check your work. Then close the open documents.

Objective 2.3: Create and manage styles

Every paragraph in a Word document is assigned a specific style. You can create an entire document that uses only the default Normal style and then modify the text and other elements with *direct formatting*, which refers to font, paragraph, and other formatting properties that are applied directly (usually by selecting the text or element and then clicking one or more formatting commands in the ribbon). Examples of direct formatting include adding bold or italic, increasing or decreasing the font size, changing the paragraph alignment, and setting the line spacing.

However, even in a document that contains only one or two levels of headings and regular paragraphs of text, you usually need to do a lot of work to give similar elements a consistent look. Styles provide much more control and consistency in how the elements of a document appear, and after you apply styles to your document, you can change a style's properties once and Word updates the style throughout the document.

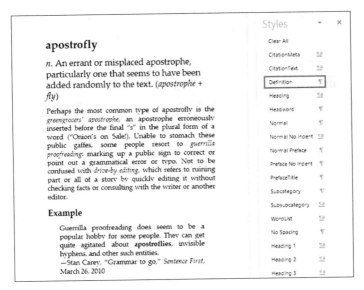

Styles maintain a consistent appearance throughout a document.

Tip To easily check which style is applied to each paragraph in a document, switch to Draft or Outline view. (You might need to increase the width of the style area pane, which you can do in the Word Options dialog box, in the Display section of the Advanced page.) Word also highlights the style applied to the selected paragraph in the Styles gallery.

This section describes how to create styles, modify an existing style—either a style you create or one of the styles defined in Word by default—and copy styles between documents.

Create paragraph and character styles

In creating a set of styles for a document or a template, you most often work with two style types:

- **Paragraph** Used to format entire paragraphs.
- **Character** Used to format one or more characters, words, phrases, or sentences within a paragraph.

Both paragraph and character styles include settings such as font, font size, and font color. Paragraph styles also include attributes for alignment, line spacing, and indentation and can include settings related to text effects, numbering, and other properties.

When you create a style, you work in the Create New Style From Formatting dialog box. If you select text and format it to reflect the style settings you want (by using options on the Home tab, in the Font and Paragraph groups, for example), the Create New Style From Formatting dialog box displays those settings when you open it.

You can use the controls in the Formatting area and the options on the Format menu to further define style attributes.

In the Properties area of the Create New Style From Formatting dialog box, you specify the style's name, the type of style you want to create, and which style the new style is based on. If you are creating a paragraph style, you can also specify the name of the existing style that you want Word to apply automatically to the following paragraph—that is, to the paragraph that Word creates when you press Enter at the end of the paragraph the new style is applied to.

Use the fields in the Properties area as follows:

- **Name** Style names are case-sensitive (MyStyle and Mystyle would be considered distinct styles), and you cannot create a style that uses the name of a style built into Word—for example, you cannot create a style named Normal (although you can modify built-in styles, as described in the next section).

- **Style type** Besides the paragraph and character types described earlier in this topic, you can also select Linked, Table, or List:
  - **Linked** When you select a linked style, Word applies the character formatting defined in a style (font color, for example, but not line spacing) or the style's full definition depending on what is selected in the document. When one or more words are selected, selecting a linked style applies the style's character formatting. Text that isn't selected is not changed and keeps the current paragraph formatting. If you select the paragraph or place the cursor within the paragraph, a linked style applies both the character and paragraph settings defined in the style.
  - **Table** You specify standard attributes such as font and paragraph settings, but you can also select settings for borders and shading and how many rows or columns (if any) are banded to display the same background.
  - **List** You can select settings for different levels. For example, you can set the top level to be numbered 1, 2, 3, with a second level identified with a, b, c, and so on.

- **Style based on** Select a style whose properties you want to use as the basis for the new style. If you base a style on the built-in Normal style, for example, and then change the font for the Normal style from Calibri to Garamond, Word also changes the font for styles based on the Normal style to Garamond.

- **Style for following paragraph** Select the style for paragraphs that follow paragraphs that use this style. Word assigns that style when you insert a paragraph break by pressing Enter. For a heading style, for example, specify Normal or another body text style in this list.

In many cases, you can capture all the formatting details you need in a paragraph style—indentation, font size, line spacing, and other such details. Within a paragraph, you can format characters by using the controls in the Font group on the Home tab or by choosing options in the Font dialog box. For more control over character formatting, you can also create styles specifically for groups of characters and then apply those styles as you format the document.

When you select Character in the Style Type list in the Create New Style From Formatting dialog box, the options in the dialog box change so that they apply only to character styles.

When you are creating a character style, the Format menu displays only formatting options relevant to character styles.

In the Style Based On list, Word displays Default Paragraph Font. Open the Style Based On list, then choose from among the built-in character styles if you want to use one of them as a starting point. In the Formatting area of the dialog box, only controls related to character formatting are available to define the style. The Format menu also restricts which formatting options you can apply to a character style.

To create a paragraph style

1. On the **Home** tab, in the **Styles** group, click the dialog box launcher in the bottom-right corner to display the **Styles** pane.

    Tip You can also toggle the Styles pane on and off by pressing Alt+Ctrl+Shift+S.

2. At the bottom of the **Styles** pane, click the **New Style** button.

Use the buttons at the bottom of the Styles pane to create and work with styles.

3. In the **Create New Style from Formatting** dialog box, define the style's properties (name, type, and others), then specify the font, font attributes, indentation, line spacing, and other settings that define the style.

4. For more detailed settings, click **Format**, choose the type of element you want to format, specify the settings you want in the relevant dialog box, and then click **OK**.

5. To save the new style in the current template, select **New documents based on this template**.

6. Click **OK** to create the style.

To create a character style

1. In the **Create New Style from Formatting** dialog box, select **Character** in the **Style type** list.

2. Use the controls in the **Formatting** area to define the attributes of the style.

3. For more detailed settings, click **Format**, choose the type of element you want to format, specify the settings you want in the relevant dialog box, and then click **OK**.

4. To save the new style in the current template, select **New documents based on this template**.

5. Click **OK** to create the style.

Modify existing styles

The basic settings that define a style include font properties (typeface, size, and color), formatting such as bold and italic, text alignment (centered, flush left, flush right, or justified), line spacing, spacing between paragraphs, and indentation. Style definitions can also include settings for character spacing, borders, and text effects such as shadows, text outlines, and fills. The styles you create and the styles defined by default in the standard Normal template are all defined by using attributes and settings such as these.

By changing these settings, you can modify a built-in style, a style you created, or a style that's defined in the template a document is based on. The Modify Style dialog box lists a style's properties in the preview area.

Select the New Documents Based On This Template option to save style changes in the template attached to the document.

Many of a style's basic settings can be modified by using the controls in the Formatting area of the Modify Style dialog box. (These settings are roughly the same as the settings in the Font and Paragraph groups on the Home tab.) The Format button at the bottom of the dialog box opens a menu with commands that lead to dialog boxes that provide options to refine settings for basic elements, including font and paragraph settings, and also to define or update settings for borders, frames, list formats, and special text effects.

Tip To select all instances of text that have a particular style applied, right-click the style either in the Styles gallery or the Styles pane, and then click Select All *X* Instance(s) (where *X* is the number of times that style has been applied in the document).

When you modify a style, be sure to review the check boxes and option buttons at the bottom of the Modify Style dialog box:

- **Add to Styles Gallery** Keep this check box selected if you have renamed a style, for example, and want it to appear in the Styles gallery on the Home tab.

- **Automatically Update** Select this check box only if you want Word to automatically modify a style's definition with any formatting changes you apply to text that the style is applied to. Those changes are reflected in all instances of the style in a document.

- **Only in This Document** Select this option if you want your style modifications to apply only to the current document.

- **New Documents Based on This Template** Select this option if you want your style modifications to be stored in the current document's template.

You can also modify an existing style by selecting text that uses the style and then formatting the text by using controls in the Font and Paragraph groups on the Home tab. When the text has the formatting you want for the style, right-click the style's name in the Styles gallery (or the Styles pane), and then click Update *Name* To Match Selection (where *Name* is the name of the style you right-clicked).

Tip In the Word Options dialog box, in the Editing Options section on the Advanced page, select Prompt To Update Style to have Word display a dialog box when you apply a style from the Styles gallery that includes updated formatting. In the dialog box, Word prompts you to update the style to include the recent changes or to reapply the formatting defined in the style.

To modify an existing style

1. In the **Styles** gallery or **Styles** pane, right-click the style, then click **Modify**.

2. In the **Modify Style** dialog box, revise the style's properties by changing the font, font attributes, indentation, line spacing, and other settings.

3. For more detailed settings, click **Format**, choose the formatting category you want to work with (such as **Font** or **Paragraph**), specify the settings you want in the relevant dialog box, and then click **OK**.

4. To save the changes to this style in the current template, select **New documents based on this template**.

5. Click **OK**.

Tip Applying styles by using keyboard shortcuts helps you format a document as you enter the document's text and other content. Word provides keyboard shortcuts for several of its built-in styles. You can assign your own keyboard shortcut to a style when you create it or when you modify the style's properties. In the Create New Style From Formatting dialog box or the Modify Style dialog box, click Format and then click Shortcut Key to open the Customize Keyboard dialog box.

Copy styles to other documents or templates

The styles that you create in one document or template can be copied or moved so that you can use them in others. By copying styles from one template or document to another, you can reuse styles, keep related templates more consistent, and cut down on the work required to define styles in each template you need. To copy specific styles from one template to another, you use the Organizer dialog box.

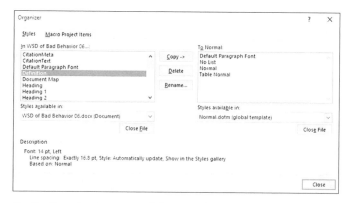

Use the Organizer to copy a style from one document or template to another.

The Organizer lists the styles defined in the templates (or documents) that you open by using the Close File and Open File buttons below the Organizer's list boxes. (You only see the Open File button after you close a file in the Organizer.) The attributes of a style you select in either list box are displayed in the Description area. Read the description to determine whether you need the style in the template to which you are copying styles. In addition to copying styles from template to template, you can delete and rename styles in the Organizer.

To copy styles between document or templates

1. Open the **Styles** pane.

2. At the bottom of the **Styles** pane, click the **Manage Styles** button.

3. In the **Manage Styles** dialog box, click **Import/Export** to display the **Styles** tab of the **Organizer**.

4. In the **Styles available in** lists, click the documents or templates you want to copy styles from and to. If the template isn't in the list, do the following:

   Click **Close File** to release the current file style list, then click **Open File** to display the content of the Templates folder.

   In the **Open** dialog box, navigate to and select the template or document you want to use, then click **Open**.

5. In the list box for the file you are copying styles from, select a style or styles, then click **Copy**.

6. When you are done copying styles, click **Close**.

Objective 2.3 practice tasks

The practice file for these tasks is located in the **MOSWordExpert2019\ Objective2** practice file folder. The folder also contains a result file that you can use to check your work.

➤ Open the **WordExpert_2-3** document, and do the following:

❑ Modify the *CitationText* style as follows:

- Add a 0.25-inch indent to the left and right.

- Change the font color to Black.

- Add top and bottom borders with a width of 1 pt.

❑ Create a paragraph style named *Book Subtitle*. Use the Cambria font set to 16 pt. and italic. Center the paragraph horizontally. Assign the keyboard shortcut Ctrl+Alt+9 to the style. (Use a different shortcut if that one is already assigned to something.) Select *Heading 1* as the style for the following paragraph.

❑ Create a paragraph style named *BookTitle*. Use 22 pt. Cambria as the font. Set the line spacing to exactly 20 pt. Set the spacing before the paragraph to 12 pt. and after the paragraph to 18 pt. Center the paragraph horizontally. Select *BookSubtitle* as the style for the following paragraph.

❑ Scroll to the top of the document. Apply the *BookTitle* style to the text *Dictionary of Bad Behavior* and the *Book Subtitle* style to the text *New Words for New Lows*.

❑ Create a character style named *DictionaryTerm*. Use Calibri, 11 pt., bold, and the Black font color as the style's attributes.

❑ Find all instances of the *Intense Emphasis* style in the document and replace them with the *DictionaryTerm* style.

➤ Open the **WordExpert_2-3_results** document. Compare the two documents to check your work. Then close the open documents.

Objective group 3

Create custom document elements

The skills tested in this section of the Microsoft Office Specialist Expert exam for Microsoft Word 365 and Microsoft Word 2019 relate to creating custom document elements. Specifically, the following objectives are associated with this set of skills:

3.1 Create and modify building blocks

3.2 Create custom design elements

3.3 Create and manage indexes

3.4 Create and manage tables of figures

Documents often have specific requirements. For example, a series of documents might require a common appearance or regularly include a content element such as a cover page or a disclaimer. You can create and save elements such as custom themes and building blocks to more efficiently work with these requirements. Business reports, academic papers, and book manuscripts are types of documents that often use references to help readers navigate the document or to meet a publisher's or an organization's requirements. Word includes features that help you create these references.

This chapter guides you in studying ways to create and modify building blocks, create custom design elements, create and manage indexes, and create and manage tables of figures.

> To complete the practice tasks in this chapter, you need the practice files contained in the **MOSWordExpert2019\Objective3** practice file folder. For more information, see "Download the practice files" in this book's Introduction.

Objective 3.1: Create and modify building blocks

Word provides building blocks for document elements such as headers and footers, cover pages, and tables. Galleries that you display by selecting commands on the ribbon are filled with these and other types of building blocks. You can create your own building blocks, save them in a gallery, and then use them again in related documents. For example, Quick Parts are a type of building block you can use to insert text or other document elements you use repeatedly. You can insert a logo or the text of a standard disclaimer in a document and then save this element to the Quick Part gallery, where it appears when you need to insert the Quick Part in a document. You can also edit the properties of building blocks.

This section describes how to create a Quick Part and edit and manage building blocks.

Create Quick Parts

Quick Parts can cover a range of elements that you use in multiple documents or repeatedly within the same document. By creating a Quick Part, you make a document element available directly from a gallery on the Insert tab. A Quick Part might contain a standard caption you use with figures or tables, a heading that is followed by placeholder text, a brief legal disclaimer, or a logo you insert at the top of correspondence or a report.

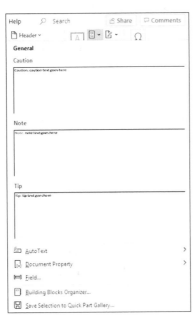

Create and save a Quick Part to add common elements to a document by using a gallery.

When you create a Quick Part (or another type of building block), you use the options in the Create New Building Block dialog box to name the Quick Part and specify other properties. By default, Word saves Quick Parts and other building blocks in a template file named *Building Blocks.dotx*. By saving a custom building block to that file (or to the standard Normal template—*Normal.dotm*), you make the building block available to all new documents. You can also save a building block in the template file attached to a document. The building block is then available to any document you create based on that template.

When you create a new building block, you can specify the following properties:

- **Name** The name of the building block. You can insert a Quick Part by typing the first several characters in its name and then pressing Enter when prompted by Word.

- **Gallery** The gallery in which you want the building block to appear. Use the built-in galleries (such as Quick Part or Cover Page) or one of the galleries Word provides named Custom. You cannot enter your own gallery name.

- **Category** You can assign a building block to a category within a gallery. Items in a gallery are grouped by their category. Select Create New Category in this list to define a custom category.

- **Description** Use this section to provide a description that appears in a Screen-Tip when you point to the building block in a gallery and when you select the item in the Building Blocks Organizer.

  > **See Also** For more information about working with the Building Blocks Organizer, see "Manage building blocks" later in this topic.

- **Save in** This box specifies the template in which to save the building block. You can select *Building Blocks.dotx* (the template used to store building blocks by default), *Normal.dotm* (the default Word template), or the template attached to the current document. Select *Building Blocks.dotx* (or *Normal.dotm*) to make the building block available to all documents. Select the template attached to the current document to create a building block specifically for that template.

- **Options** These options specify how the building block is inserted. The choices are Insert Content Only, Insert Content In Its Own Paragraph, and Insert Content In Its Own Page. The first of these choices places the building block at the cursor without adding a paragraph or page break.

3

To create a Quick Part

1. Select the content you want to include in the Quick Part.

2. On the **Insert** tab, in the **Text** group, click **Quick Parts**, then click **Save Selection to Quick Part Gallery**.

3. In the **Create New Building Block** dialog box, enter a name and a description for the Quick Part.

4. Select the gallery and category in which you want the Quick Part to appear.

5. In the **Save in** list, do either of the following:

   - To make the Quick Part available to all documents, click **Building Blocks.dotx**.

   - To include the Quick Part only in the template attached to the document, click that template.

Saving the Quick Part to Building Blocks.dotx makes it available to all new documents.

6. In the **Options** list, select the option you want to use to insert the Quick Part: **Insert content only**, **Insert content in its own paragraph**, or **Insert content in its own page**.

7. Click **OK** to apply the settings.

To insert a Quick Part in a document

→ Enter the name of the Quick Part, then press **F3**.

Or

1. On the **Insert** tab, in the **Text** group, click **Quick Parts**.

2. In the **Quick Parts** gallery, do one of the following:

    -   Click a Quick Part to insert it by using the default insertion option.

    -   Right-click a Quick Part, then click one of the following insertion options:

        -   **Insert at Current Document Position**

        -   **Insert at Page Header**

        -   **Insert at Page Footer**

        -   **Insert at Beginning of Section**

        -   **Insert at End of Section**

        -   **Insert at Beginning of Document**

        -   **Insert at End of Document**

Manage building blocks

You can view the range of building blocks that come with Word by displaying galleries (such as for cover pages or watermarks) from the ribbon. In addition, Word displays the list of building blocks in the Building Blocks Organizer, a dialog box you can open by clicking Quick Parts on the Insert tab and then clicking Building Blocks Organizer. Select a building block in the list to display a preview and a description. You can then modify the properties of the selected building block and remove building blocks you no longer need.

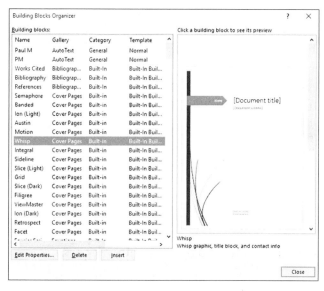

Sort and move building blocks from the Organizer.

Each building block is defined by a set of properties that you can use to keep building blocks organized and to specify how Word inserts the building block. In the Modify Building Block dialog box, you can change the gallery a building block is assigned to, update its category, modify its description, and change other properties.

See Also For a detailed description of building block properties, see "Create Quick Parts" earlier in this topic.

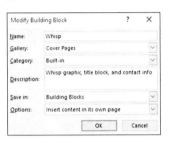

Modify a building block to save it in a different location or in a different category.

To open the Building Blocks Organizer

→ On the **Insert** tab, in the **Text** group, click **Quick Parts**, then click **Building Blocks Organizer**.

→ In the **Quick Parts** gallery, right-click a building block, then click **Organize and Delete**.

To open the Modify Building Block dialog box for a building block

→ In the **Quick Parts** gallery, right-click the building block you want to modify, then click **Edit Properties**.

→ Open the **Building Blocks Organizer**. In the **Building blocks** pane, click the building block you want to modify, then click **Edit Properties**.

To edit building block properties

1. Open the **Modify Building Block** dialog box for the building block that you want to modify.

2. Update the **Name**, **Gallery**, **Category**, **Description**, **Save In**, or **Options** properties, then click **OK**.

3. When Word prompts you to redefine the building block entry, click **Yes**.

To delete a building block

1. Open the **Building Blocks Organizer**.

2. In the **Building blocks** pane, click the building block you want to delete.

3. Below the **Building blocks** pane, click **Delete**.

4. When Word prompts you to confirm the deletion, click **Yes**.

3

Objective 3.1 practice tasks

The practice file for these tasks is located in the **MOSWordExpert2019\Objective3** practice file folder.

➤ Open the **WordExpert_3-1** document, and do the following:

❏ Create a Quick Part from the "Tip: Tip text goes here" line of the document. Name the Quick Part *Tip*, add the description *Inserts a Tip element*, select the option Insert Content In Its Own Paragraph, and accept the other defaults.

❏ Create a Quick Part from the "Note: Note text goes here" line of the document. Name the Quick Part *Note*, add the description *Inserts a Note element*, select the option Insert Content In Its Own Paragraph, and accept the other defaults.

❏ Create a Quick Part from the "Caution: Caution text goes here" line of the document. Name the Quick Part *Caution*, add the description *Inserts a Caution element*, select the option Insert Content In Its Own Paragraph, and accept the other defaults.

❏ Open the Building Blocks Organizer. For the Tip, Note, and Caution Quick Parts in turn, move the Quick Part to a custom category named *Sidebar building blocks*.

➤ Save the **WordExpert_3-1** document, then close the document. (Note that there is no results file for these practice tasks since building blocks are not stored within a regular Word document, as described earlier in this topic.)

Objective 3.2: Create custom design elements

Themes and styles provide ways to consistently format the content of a Word document. Themes specify default fonts for body and heading text, colors for headings and other elements, and text effects such as shadows. Styles specify settings for fonts, paragraphs, tabs, and other formatting that are applied as a group to paragraphs and characters. Style sets provide a means of changing the appearance of multiple styles at one time. This topic describes how to create custom color and font sets, custom themes, and custom style sets.

See Also For more information about styles, see "Objective 2.3: Create and manage styles."

When you work with themes, styles, and style sets, keep in mind that a template is defined (in part) by the styles it contains and the attributes for those styles. After you apply styles to the content of your document, you can apply a different template or style set to update styles with the same name to reflect the formatting defined in the new template or style set. If the styles in a template or a document are set up to use theme fonts and theme colors, you can display a different set of fonts and colors by applying a new theme.

You manage themes and style sets by using commands in the Document Formatting group on the Design tab.

Create custom color sets

Word offers many tools for turning a plain, unformatted file into an attractive, professional-quality document. For example, features such as cover pages and Word's numerous typography tools can make your document easy to read. The final touch involves adding just the right amount of color to your text. With colors, you can emphasize important results, shape the layout of your page, and add subtle psychological effects. Word comes with nearly two dozen built-in color sets (also called color themes) that make it easy to apply colors to your documents.

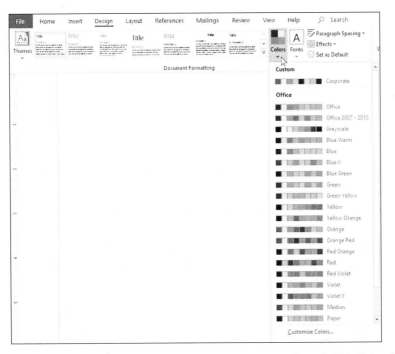

Custom color sets appear at the top of the Theme Colors menu, above the 23 built-in color sets in the Office gallery.

However, if no scheme offers the exact colors you want, you can create your own. Each scheme consists of 12 color elements:

- **Text/Background - Dark 1** The dark text color that Word applies when you choose a light background color
- **Text/Background - Light 1** The light text color that Word applies when you choose a dark background color
- **Text/Background - Dark 2** The dark background color that Word applies when you choose a light text color
- **Text/Background - Light 2** The light background color that Word applies when you choose a dark text color
- **Accent 1 through Accent 6** The colors that Word uses for accents, such as chart data markers

■ **Hyperlink and Followed Hyperlink** The colors that Word uses for worksheet links: the former for links that haven't been clicked and the latter for links that have been clicked

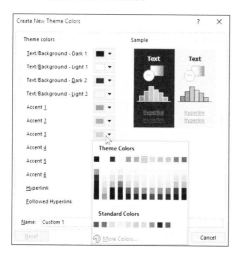

To create a custom color scheme, you can replace any of the dozen theme colors with an existing theme color, a standard color, or a custom color.

For each element, you can choose a color from Word's standard color palette, or you can create a custom color. Word offers two color models:

■ **RGB** This color model is based on the idea that you can create any color by combining three base colors: red, green, and blue. You assign a value between 0 and 255 for each color: the higher the number, the more intense the color.

> **Tip** In the RGB color model, when the red, green, and blue values are equal, you get a grayscale color. Lower numbers produce darker grays, and higher numbers produce lighter grays. Black has RGB values of 0, 0, 0 and white has RGB values of 255, 255, 255.

■ **HSL** This color model is based on three properties, each of which is assigned a value between 0 and 255:

- *Hue* (which is more or less equivalent to the term *color*) measures the position on the color spectrum. Lower numbers indicate a position near the red end, and higher numbers move through the yellow, green, blue, and violet parts of the spectrum.

- *Saturation* is a measure of the purity of a particular hue, with 255 giving a pure color and lower numbers indicating that more gray is mixed with the hue until, at 0, the color becomes part of the gray scale.

- *Luminance* is a measure of the brightness of a color, where lower numbers are darker and higher numbers are brighter.

Drag horizontally to set the hue, or vertically to set the saturation

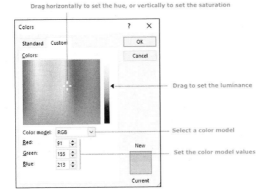

On the Custom tab, you can either specify RGB or HSL values, or you can drag the color pointer and the luminance slider.

To create a custom color set

1. On the **Design** tab, in the **Document Formatting** group, click **Colors**, then click **Customize Colors**.

Tip If an existing color set is close to what you want, you can save some time and effort by using that color set as your starting point. On the Design tab, in the Document Formatting groups, click Colors, and then click the color set to apply it to the document and use it as the starting point.

---

2. For any theme color you want to modify, click the color picker to display a menu of color options, then do one of the following:

- In the **Theme Colors** gallery, click one of the 12 existing theme colors or 60 variations to assign it to the color role.

- In the **Standard Colors** gallery, click one of the 10 standard colors.

- Click **More Colors** to open the **Colors** dialog box. On the **Custom** tab, in the **Color model** list, select either **RGB** or **HSL**, do any of the following, and then click **OK**:

  - If you chose **RGB**, enter specific values for **Red**, **Green**, and **Blue**.

  - If you chose **HSL**, enter specific values for **Hue**, **Sat**, and **Lum**.

  - To adjust the hue visually, drag the color pointer horizontally.

  - To adjust the saturation visually, drag the color pointer vertically.

  - To adjust the luminance visually, drag the luminance slider.

3. Repeat step 2 for each theme color you want to modify.

4. In the **Name** box, enter a name for your new color set.

5. Click **Save** to save the color set and apply it to the document.

Create custom font sets

Each Word theme comes with more than two dozen built-in font sets that make it easy to apply fonts to your documents. Each font set defines two fonts:

- A *Heading font* that Word uses for title and heading text
- A *Body font* that Word uses for regular document text

The typeface is often the same for both types of text, but some font sets use two different typefaces, such as Calibri Light for titles and headings and Calibri for body text. If no existing font set includes the typefaces you want, you can create your own.

A custom font set can include any installed fonts.

To create a custom font set

1. On the **Design** tab, in the **Document Formatting** group, click **Fonts**, then click **Customize Fonts**.

2. In the **Heading font** list, select a font for worksheet headings.

3. In the **Body font** list, select a font for worksheet text.

4. In the **Name** box, enter a name for your new font set.

5. Click **Save** to save the font set and close the dialog box.

Create custom themes

A *theme* is a predefined collection of color, font, and effect formatting options. Each theme comes with preset formatting in three categories: color scheme, font set, and effects (which include formatting such as drop shadows and 3D effects). Word offers more than three dozen predefined themes.

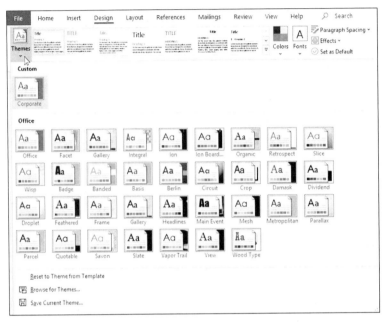

Custom themes appear at the top of the Themes menu, above the 34 built-in themes in the Office gallery.

If none of the predefined themes offer the exact formatting you require, you can modify any theme by selecting a different color scheme, font set, or effects scheme. You can even create your own custom color and font sets. However, if you go to all this trouble to get your workbook formatting just right, it is time-consuming to have to repeat the same steps for other workbooks you open or create. To avoid this problem, you can save your theme customizations as a new workbook theme. This enables you to apply the custom formatting to any workbook just by selecting the custom theme.

Exam Strategy The objective domain for Exam MO-101, "Microsoft Word Expert (Word and Word 2019)," requires you to demonstrate the ability to create custom color schemes, font sets, and themes. You will not be required to customize effect schemes.

To create a custom theme

1. In the active document, create or apply the color set, font set, paragraph spacing, and effects you want to include in the theme.

2. On the **Design** tab, click **Themes**, then select **Save Current Theme** to open the **Save Current Theme** dialog box.

> **IMPORTANT** By default, Word displays the Document Themes folder, which is located in your user profile's AppData\Roaming\Microsoft\Templates folder. Save your theme in this folder to ensure that it gets displayed in the Themes list.

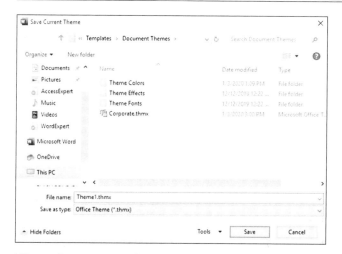

When saving your custom theme, be sure to store it in the Document Themes folder.

3. In the **File name** box, enter a name for the custom theme.

4. Click **Save**.

Create custom style sets

Style sets are like themes; they can change the overall appearance of a document in a single step. In addition to fonts and colors, style sets can change character attributes such as font size and capitalization, and paragraph attributes such as line spacing, borders, and alignment. The use of style sets reinforces the advantages of applying defined styles to distinct document elements (headings, lists, and normal paragraphs, for example). With styles in place in a document, you can change the look of a document by applying a different style set.

> **IMPORTANT** Style sets change only formatting defined by styles. Any formatting applied directly to a document element is not updated by applying a style set.

A style set's definitions are contained in a .dotx file, the file name extension used for Word templates. However, applying a style set does not replace the template associated with a document; it only applies the style set's style definitions. If, after applying a style set, you want to restore the formatting defined in the current template, you can revert to using the style definitions included in that template by clicking the Reset command at the bottom of the Style Set gallery.

When you create and save a custom style set, Word prompts you to save the file in your user profile, at C:\Users*user name*\AppData\Roaming\Microsoft\QuickStyles.

> **See Also** For more information about modifying styles, see "Modify existing styles" in "Objective 2.3: Create and manage styles."

To create a custom style set

1. Set up a document with the style definitions you want to use. (Start with an existing style set if you want to.)

2. On the **Design** tab, in the **Document Formatting** group, click the **More** button to open the **Style Set** menu, then click **Save as a New Style Set**.

3. In the **Save as a New Style Set** dialog box, name the style set, then click **Save**.

Objective 3.2 practice tasks

The practice file for these tasks is located in the **MOSWordExpert2019\ Objective3** practice file folder. The folder also contains result files that you can use to check your work.

➤ Open the **WordExpert_3-2a** document, and do the following:

❑ Apply the *Savon* theme to the document.

❑ Apply the built-in *Green Yellow* theme color set to the document.

❑ Apply the built-in *Consolas-Verdana* theme font set to the document.

❑ Observe how the font is applied to different elements and how the fonts change.

❑ Create a custom color set named ***WordExpertColors.*** Select *Dark Green* as the Accent 1 color.

❑ Create a custom font set named ***WordExpertFonts.*** Select *Corbel* as the heading font and *Bookman Old Style* as the body font.

❑ Observe how the font set is applied to different elements and how the fonts change.

❑ Apply the built-in *Black & White (Capitalized)* style set to the document and observe the changes.

❑ Modify the *Heading 1* style to use a font size of 24 pt., with a bold italic style.

❑ Modify the *Normal* style to use the Times New Roman font. Set the paragraph spacing to 12 pt. after. Save the changes as a custom style set named ***WordExpertStyleSet.***

➤ Save the **WordExpert_3-2a** document.

➤ Open the **WordExpert_3-2a_results** document. Compare the two documents to check your work. Then close the open documents.

➤ Open the **WordExpert_3-2b** document.

❑ Apply the *WordExpertColors* custom color set.

❑ Apply the *WordExpertFonts* custom font set.

❑ Apply the *WordExpertStyleSet* custom style set.

➤ Save the **WordExpert_3-2b document**.

➤ Open the **WordExpert_3-2b_results** document. Compare the two documents to check your work. Then close the open documents.

Objective 3.3: Create and manage indexes

A savvy buyer of nonfiction will examine a book's index before deciding whether to purchase the book, and a savvy user of nonfiction will make regular use of a book's index after buying it. In almost all nonfiction books, a good index is an essential feature.

Is an index essential in your Word documents? That depends on several factors:

- **Length** The longer the document, the more likely an index is necessary or expected.

- **Complexity** The more complex a document's subject matter, the more likely an index helps cut through that complexity and enables your readers to find what they want.

- **Audience** Some people simply expect an index and are inordinately upset if a document does not include one.

If you have a document that has some or all of these factors, then you ought to consider adding an index. However, I should mention early on that creating an index is tedious, time-consuming, and finicky work. Although some techniques are available that you can use to lighten the load, you should not make the decision to include an index lightly. Finally, although building a quality index for a large document such as a book requires special training, Word's indexing tools are all you really need for more modest projects.

3

Before you add an index to a document, you need to complete two general steps: mark index entries (by inserting index fields) and set options for how Word generates the index. Word uses the entries and the options you specify to create the index, assigning page numbers to the entries based on their location in the document.

An example of a completed index, with main entries and indented subentries.

You can use several approaches to mark index entries:

- Select the text you want to use as an entry.

- Add an entry of your own at the location where you want the index marker.

- Compile terms in a separate file, and have Word insert index markers based on the terms in the file.

An index entry must define at least one level, the main entry. Index entries can also include subentries and cross-references to other entries in the index. Entries can refer to a specific page or to a range of pages. For example, a main entry of *macros* might include subentries such as *recording*, *editing*, and *assigning to a button*. The page reference for the main entry might span several pages, with subentries covered on a single page or a span of fewer pages.

Mark index entries

When you insert entries manually by selecting or entering text, you work in the Mark Index Entry dialog box. If text is selected when you open the Mark Index Entry dialog box, that text is displayed in the Main Entry box. You can keep the Mark Index Entry dialog box open as you work on a document. Text that is selected when you click the dialog box to make it active replaces any text currently in the Main Entry box. You don't need to select text to create a main entry, however. You can define a main entry yourself by clicking where you want an index reference placed in the document and then entering the text in the Main Entry box.

To reference content that spans multiple pages, define a bookmark and point the index entry to the bookmark.

Tip You can apply formatting such as bold, italic, and underline to the text in the Main Entry, Subentry, and Cross-Reference boxes by selecting the text and then using the formatting keyboard shortcuts. For example, you might need to italicize the title of a book or journal or choose to display in bold terms that also appear in a glossary. The formatting you apply by using the formatting keyboard shortcuts does not override settings for index styles defined in the template attached to the document.

Subentries for a main entry must be entered manually. You can also create a third-level entry within the subentry or create a cross-reference (such as a *See* reference) to other index entries as needed.

Word defines index entries within hidden index fields. An index field is identified by the characters *XE*. Curly braces enclose the index field tag and text.

Tip If index fields are not displayed in your document, display hidden formatting marks.

Here is an example of the information that an index field might contain:

{ XE "formatting:characters: font" \t "See also styles" }

An entry that spans a range of pages is associated with a bookmark that you define in the document. The bookmark is associated with the content that you want the index entry to refer to. The bookmark does not identify specific page numbers itself. The indexing feature in Word assigns page numbers to the bookmarked range when you generate the index.

The Mark All button in the Mark Index Entry dialog box inserts an index field at the first occurrence of the main entry in each paragraph of the document. For example, if the main entry is *styles*, clicking Mark All inserts an index field for the first occurrence of the word *styles* in each paragraph of the document. If you use the Mark All button, keep in mind that Word distinguishes between uppercase and lowercase occurrences of a term—in the previous example, occurrences of *Styles* would not be marked.

To display index entries and hidden formatting symbols in a document

→ On the **Home** tab, in the **Paragraph** group, click **Show/Hide ¶**.

To open the Mark Index Entry dialog box

→ On the **References** tab, in the **Index** group, click **Mark Entry**.

→ Press **Alt+Shift+X**.

To mark index entries

1. Open the **Mark Index Entry** dialog box.

2. In the document, do either of the following:

   • Select the text for which you want to create a main index entry, then click the **Mark Index Entry** dialog box to make it active.

   • Click where you want an index marker to be in the document, and then in the **Mark Index Entry** dialog box, enter the text for the entry in the **Main Entry** box.

3. If you want to define a second-level index term, enter the term in the **Subentry** box. If you want to define a third-level entry, add a colon to the end of the sub-entry, then enter the third-level term.

4. In the **Options** area, do one of the following:

   • Click **Cross-reference**, then enter the text for the reference.

   • Click **Current page**.

   • Click **Page range**, then select the bookmark for the range of pages the entry is related to.

   > **See Also** For information about bookmarking page ranges, see the next procedure.

5. In the **Page number format** area, if you want Word to apply specific formatting to the page number, select the **Bold** and/or **Italic** check box.

6. Do either of the following:

   • To insert a single index entry in the current location, click **Mark.**

   • To insert an index entry for the first instance of the term in each paragraph of the document, be sure the **Current page** option is selected, then click **Mark All**.

To create a bookmark that defines a page range

1. Select the paragraphs you want to include in the page range.

2. On the **Insert** tab, in the **Links** group, click **Bookmark**.

3. In the **Bookmark** dialog box, enter a name for the bookmark, then click **Add**.

Insert index entries from a file

You can create an index by maintaining a file that contains main entries in a separate document (also referred to as an *automark file* or a *concordance file*) that Word uses to mark entries in the document being indexed. The automark file can be saved as a Word document or in other formats, such as a text (.txt) file. Each entry is set up as a separate paragraph. Word then searches for each term or phrase in the automark file and inserts a corresponding index field for the first instance of the term or phrase it finds in each paragraph of the document.

For more flexibility, you can set up the list in a two-column table, with the terms you want to search for in the left column and the corresponding index entries in the right column. By using two columns, you can collect terms such as *format*, *formatting*, and *formatted* under the same main entry—list the terms separately in the table's left column and enter the same main entry in the table's right column.

The entries in an automark file are case-sensitive. For example, if the automark file includes the term *text effects*, Word won't insert an index field for an instance of *Text effects* when it indexes the document.

To create an automark file

1. In a blank document, do one of the following:

    - Enter the index terms in individual paragraphs.

    - Create a two-column table. Enter terms that you want Word to index in the first column, and the index tags you want to associate with each term in the second column.

2. Save the file.

To mark index entries by using an automark file

1. On the **References** tab, in the **Index** group, click **Insert Index**.

2. In the **Index** dialog box, click **AutoMark**.

3. In the **Open Index AutoMark File** dialog box, browse to and select the automark file, then click **Open**.

Create and update indexes

After you mark index entries, you use the options in the Index dialog box to specify the index's design and other options for the appearance of the index.

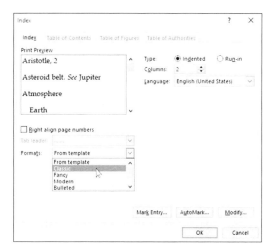

Choose a preset index format from the Formats list.

Word supports two index formats: indented and run-in. By default, both formats appear in a two-column layout and are wrapped to fit the width of the columns. In an indented index, the entries are listed in this format:

> *Styles*
> > *applying, 211*
> >
> > *creating, 209*
> >
> > *updating in template, 212*

In a run-in index, an entry would appear as follows:

> *Styles: applying, 211; creating, 209; updating in template, 212*

A run-in index saves space, which makes it a good choice if you have only a limited number of pages for the index. When you select an option for the type of index, Word displays an example in the Print Preview area of the Index dialog box.

You can change the number of columns (from 1 through 4) or set the Columns box to Auto (in which case the index uses the same number of columns as defined in the document). If you are using an indented index, you can change the alignment of page numbers. Word previews this format when you select the option, and you can then select the type of tab leader you want to include (or select None from this list). The Formats list provides several options for styling the fonts, line spacing, and other formats Word applies to the index entries when you generate the index.

Tip If From Template is selected in the Formats list, you can modify the styles for index levels. Click Modify in the Index dialog box. In the Style dialog box, select an index level, then click Modify to open the Modify Style dialog box and make changes to the formatting attributes for that index level. For more information about modifying styles, see "Objective 2.3: Create and manage styles."

If you need to edit an index entry, you should edit the specific index field and not the index that Word generates. By editing the entry, you ensure that corrections are included if you generate the index again. Locate the field in the document, and then edit and format the text enclosed in quotation marks within the curly braces that define the field.

After you make changes to index markers, you can update the index in place.

Tip When editing index entries, you can move between fields by using the search features on the Find and Go To tabs of the Find And Replace dialog box. To locate fields from the Find tab, click Field in the Special list. To locate fields from the Go To tab, click Field in the Go To What list.

To specify index formatting options and generate the index

1. In the document, click where you want to insert the index.

2. On the **References** tab, in the **Index** group, click **Insert Index**.

3. In the **Index** dialog box, set the following options, then click **OK**:

   - In the **Type** area, click **Indented** or **Run-in**.

   - In the **Columns** box, enter or select the number of columns you want to arrange the index entries in.

   - If you are using a language other than the default language on your system, choose a language.

- If you are using an indented index, select the **Right align page numbers** check box, then select the style of tab leader you want to use.

- Select a format for the index, or keep **From template** selected.

To edit index entries

1. In the document, display index entries and hidden formatting symbols.

2. Locate the index entry you want to edit, and edit the text within the index tag.

To delete index entries

1. In the document, display index entries and hidden formatting symbols.

2. Locate the index entry you want to delete.

3. Select the entire field (including the curly braces), then press the **Delete** key.

To update an index

→ Click anywhere in the index, and then, on the **References** tab, in the **Index** group, click **Update Index**.

→ Right-click the index, then click **Update Field**.

3

Objective 3.3 practice tasks

The practice file for these tasks is located in the **MOSWordExpert2019\ Objective3** practice file folder. The folder also contains result files that you can use to check your work.

➤ Open the **WordExpert_3-3a** document and do the following:

☐ Define a bookmark that starts with the section heading "Word's formatting buttons" and includes the whole section. Name the bookmark ***formatting_buttons***.

☐ Define a bookmark that starts with the section heading "Formatting from the keyboard" and includes the whole section. Name the bookmark ***keyboard_formatting***.

☐ Work through the file and add index entries for the following terms:

character formatting

Create New Style from Formatting dialog box

Font group

Format Painter

formatting

Home tab

Mini Toolbar

paragraph formatting

Paragraph group

styles

Styles gallery

☐ After the heading "Word's formatting buttons," insert a main entry for *formatting* and a subentry for *buttons*. Use the bookmark named *formatting_buttons* to indicate the page range.

❑ After the heading "Formatting from the keyboard," insert a main entry for *formatting* and a subentry for *keystrokes*. Use the bookmark named *keyboard_formatting* to indicate the page range.

❑ After the heading "Working with the Mini Toolbar," insert a main entry for *formatting* and a subentry for *Mini Toolbar*.

❑ After the heading "Using the Format Painter," insert a main entry for *formatting* and a subentry for *Format Painter*.

❑ In the section "Understanding formatting," after the text "Here are the three main types of formatting," insert a main entry for *formatting* and a subentry for *types*.

❑ In the section "Understanding formatting," after the text "Here are the two main methods for applying character and paragraph formatting," insert a main entry for *formatting* and a subentry for *methods*.

❑ Generate a run-in index, placing the index at the end of the document.

❑ Find the entries for *formatting* and edit the entries so that they read *formatting text*.

❑ Update the index to reflect your changes.

➤ Save the **WordExpert_3-3a** document.

➤ Open the **WordExpert_3-3a_results** document. Compare the two documents to check your work. (The number of entries and their placement in your document might differ from those shown in the result file.) When you are done, close the open documents.

➤ Open the **WordExpert_3-3b** document and do the following:

❑ In the blank document, create an automark file listing the same terms provided in the earlier list, pressing Enter after each term.

➤ Save the **WordExpert_3-3b** document.

➤ Open the **WordExpert_3-3b_results** document. Compare the two documents to check your work. Then close the open documents.

➤ Open the **WordExpert_3-3c** document and do the following:

❑ Insert index entries by referencing the **WordExpert_3-3b** automark file.

❑ Generate an indented index, placing it at the end of the document.

➤ Save the **WordExpert_3-3c** document.

➤ Open the **WordExpert_3-3c_results** document. Compare the two documents to check your work. Then close the open documents.

Objective 3.4: Create and manage tables of figures

Descriptive captions are used to identify document elements such as illustrations, charts, tables, code listings, and equations. After captions are associated with a set of objects, you can generate a reference table that lists the captions and their positions within the document. A *table of figures* (TOF) is most commonly a listing of the figures or illustrations in a document, and it usually appears just after the table of contents (TOC). Like a TOC, the TOF can also include page numbers and you can set up each TOF entry as a hyperlink. You can also create separate TOFs for a document's tables, charts, equations, and so on. When you define a caption, you associate it with a specific element (a label) and can set options for how similar elements are numbered and how captions are positioned. Word applies its built-in Caption style to the captions you create.

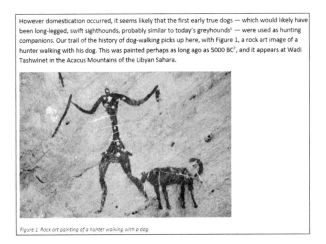

However domestication occurred, it seems likely that the first early true dogs — which would likely have been long-legged, swift sighthounds, probably similar to today's greyhounds[6] — were used as hunting companions. Our trail of the history of dog-walking picks up here, with Figure 1, a rock art image of a hunter walking with his dog. This was painted perhaps as long ago as 5000 BC[7], and it appears at Wadi Tashwinet in the Acacus Mountains of the Libyan Sahara.

Figure 1 Rock art painting of a hunter walking with a dog

Add a caption to document elements such as figures and tables.

The Insert Caption command in the Reference tab's Captions group opens the dialog box in which you enter a caption and define settings for how Word displays it.

Use one of the default labels, or create your own.

Referring to the Caption text box, you can see that a caption has three parts:

- **Caption label** The type of element, such as a figure or table. In our example, the caption label is *Figure*.

- **Caption number** The instance of the element in the document (where 1 refers to the first instance, 2 to the second instance, and so on). In our example, the caption number is *1*.

- **Caption text** The description of the element. In our example, the text is *Rock art painting of a hunter walking with a dog*.

In the Caption dialog box, use the Label list to select the type of element you are adding a caption to. The default choices are Equation, Figure, and Table. You can define captions for other document elements (charts or maps, for example). You can delete custom labels when you no longer need them, but you cannot delete the default labels.

By clicking the Numbering button, you open the Caption Numbering dialog box. You can use the options in this dialog box to switch to a different numbering format (such as Roman numerals) or to include a chapter number with a caption's label (for example, Table 3-3). Chapter headings must be defined by using one of the built-in heading styles. You can also select a character to separate the chapter number and the figure or table number. A hyphen is used by default; other choices include a period or a colon.

Tip If you often insert the same type of object in a document and you want these objects to have captions, click AutoCaption in the Caption dialog box. Select the type of object (such as Bitmap Image or Microsoft Excel Worksheet) that you want Word to provide a caption for when you insert an object of this type. You can select the label that's used with specific object types (or create a new label), where Word positions the caption by default, and specify how captions for this type of object are numbered.

If you need to modify a caption, you can edit the caption text directly in the document or select the caption (including the label and number) and edit the caption in the Caption dialog box. With the Caption dialog box open, you can select a different label if needed, create a new label, or modify the numbering scheme for the captioned objects.

You can insert a table of figures to display a list of document elements with captions—tables, figures, equations, or elements you've added captions to that are associated with a label you defined. Word generates the table of figures from the captions associated with these objects.

The steps and options for creating a table of figures are like those for a table of contents. The Table Of Figures dialog box previews how Word will display the table in a printed document and online. You can choose a built-in format or use the style defined in the current template.

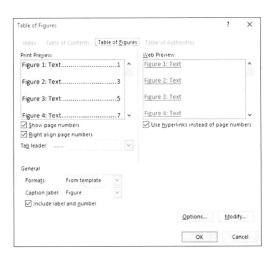

Use the Table Of Figures dialog box to create reference tables for figures, tables, and other captioned elements.

In the Caption Label list, you select the label for the type of element you want to display in the table of figures. You can select None (in which case, numbered entries are preceded by *Caption*), Figure, Table, Equation, or a custom label you define by using the Caption dialog box.

By default, Word uses its built-in Caption style and the associated label to create the table of figures. Any element to which that style is applied and that is identified with that label is included. In the Table Of Figures Options dialog box, you can select a style to use as the basis for the entries in the table of figures or use table entries you have defined manually. As you can with table of content styles, you can modify the styles Word uses to display the table of figures.

To insert a caption for a document element

1. Select the object you want to create a caption for.

2. On the **References** tab, in the **Captions** group, click **Insert Caption**.

3. In the **Caption** dialog box, in the **Label** list, select the type of object.

4. In the **Caption** box, enter the caption after the label.

5. In the **Position** list, select an option for where you want to insert the caption.

IMPORTANT The Position list is available only if you selected an object before opening the Caption dialog box.

---

6. Click **Numbering** to open the **Caption Numbering** dialog box, then adjust number formatting for the caption.

7. Click **OK** in each of the open dialog boxes.

To create a custom label

1. On the **References** tab, in the **Captions** group, click **Insert Caption**.

2. In the **Caption** dialog box, click **New Label**.

3. Enter a name for the label, then click **OK**.

To insert a table of figures

1. Click where you want to insert the table of figures.

2. On the **References** tab, in the **Captions** group, click **Insert Table of Figures**.

3. In the **Table of Figures** dialog box, set options for showing and aligning page numbers and choose the tab leader character and a table of figures format.

4. In the **Caption label** list, select the label you want to include with the captions.

5. If you want to remove hyperlinks from the table of figure entries, clear the **Use hyperlinks instead of page numbers** check box.

6. Click **OK** to insert the table of figures.

To set options for a table of figures

1. In the **Table of Figures** dialog box, click **Options**.

2. In the **Table of Figures Options** dialog box, do either of the following:

   • To base the table on a different style, select **Style**, then choose a style from the list.

   • To include manually marked table entries, select **Table entry fields**.

3. Click **OK** in each of the open dialog boxes to insert the table.

Objective 3.4 practice tasks

The practice file for these tasks is located in the **MOSWordExpert2019\Objective3** practice file folder. The folder also contains a result file that you can use to check your work.

➤ Open the **WordExpert_3-4** document and do the following:

❑ In the first blank paragraph after each table, insert a caption using the built-in *Table* label. Accept the other default caption settings.

❑ In the blank paragraph after the *Tables* heading, insert a table of figures that references the table captions.

❑ In the blank paragraph after each picture, insert a caption that uses a custom Image label named *Screenshot*. Accept the other default caption settings.

❑ In the blank paragraph after the *Screenshots* heading, insert a table of figures that references the image captions.

➤ Save the **WordExpert_3-4** document.

➤ Open the **WordExpert_3-4_results** document. Compare the two documents to check your work. Then close the open documents.

Objective group 4

Use advanced Word features

The skills tested in this section of the Microsoft Office Specialist Expert exam for Microsoft Word 365 and Microsoft Word 2019 relate to working some of Word's advanced features. Specifically, the following objectives are associated with this set of skills:

- **4.1** Manage forms, fields, and controls
- **4.2** Create and modify macros
- **4.3** Perform mail merges

Word also provides tools that you can use to produce bulk mailings or to capture specific document information by using fields.

This chapter guides you in studying methods for building forms, inserting fields, adding controls, creating and modifying VBA macros, and performing mail merge operations.

To complete the practice tasks in this chapter, you need the practice files contained in the **MOSWordExpert2019\Objective4** practice file folder. For more information, see "Download the practice files" in this book's Introduction.

Objective 4.1: Manage forms, fields, and controls

In specific types of documents, especially forms, you can add and define content controls to manage input and data collection. Content controls such as list boxes or combo boxes are similar to the types of controls that appear regularly in dialog boxes. This section also describes how to insert fields to display information about a document or to automate information that is contained in document elements such as headers or footers.

Insert and configure content controls

To help build documents that capture user input (forms, for example), you can insert and configure a variety of content controls, including text boxes, check boxes, and date pickers. You use content controls to manage input by specifying items for a list, for example, or by providing a defined set of options related to check boxes.

Content controls display a simple text statement that tells users what to do with the control. For example, text controls display *Click or tap here to enter text*, and the date picker control prompts users to *Click or tap to enter a date*. You can customize this text so that it provides precise instructions and helps users work with a control more efficiently.

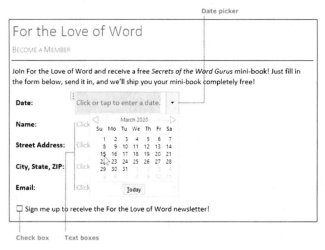

A document that contains multiple content controls.

The content controls you can add to a document are displayed in the Controls group on the Developer tab. The following content controls are available:

> **See Also** The Developer tab is hidden by default. To learn how to display the Developer tab, see "Display hidden ribbon tabs" in "Objective 1.1: Manage documents and templates."

- **Rich text** Use this control for text fields in which you need to format text as bold or italic, for example, or if you need to include multiple paragraphs and add other content such as images and tables.

- **Plain text** Use the plain-text control for simple text fields such as names, addresses, or job titles. The text added to a plain-text control can be formatted only in limited ways, and the control can include only a single paragraph by default.

- **Picture** Use this control to embed an image file in a document. You can use a picture control to display a logo, for example, or pictures of project personnel.

- **Building block gallery** Use a building block gallery control when you want users of the document to have access to a specific block of text saved as a Quick Part or to AutoText entries, equations, or tables from those respective building block galleries. You can also select a custom gallery. In a request for proposal document, for example, you might include a building block control from which users choose text entries from the Quick Parts gallery to indicate the length of time for which the proposal is valid. You choose which gallery the content control is associated with in the properties dialog box for the control.

> **See Also** For more information about building blocks, see "Create Quick Parts" and "Manage building blocks" in "Objective 3.1: Create and modify building blocks." For information about control properties, read further in this section.

- **Check box** Use the check box control to provide an option that can be either on (the check box is selected) or off (the check box is cleared).

- **Combo box** In a combo box, users can select from a list of defined choices or enter their own information. If you lock a combo box control, users cannot add their own items to the list.

> **See Also** For more information about locking controls, read further in this section.

4

- **Drop-down list** In this control, users can select only from a list of defined options. You might use a drop-down list to display department names, meeting rooms, or product names (a list of specific items). A combo box is better suited for displaying a list of tasks so that users can select a task if it appears on the list or define one if it doesn't.

- **Date picker** This control inserts a calendar control that lets users select or enter a date.

- **Repeating section** A repeating section content control can guide readers in entering the same information in multiple sections. You can also nest other content controls (such as a text box) within a repeating section control. You could use this content control in a table, for example, to alert users of a document about what information should be inserted in each column and in each row.

Document content controls.

Tip Pointing to a content control in the Controls group on the Developer tab displays a ScreenTip that identifies the control.

Tip To group content controls, select the controls, and then click Group in the Controls group on the Developer tab. For example, you can group a set of check boxes so that they cannot be edited or deleted individually.

Each content control has a set of properties. The most basic properties are Title and Tag. Word displays a control's title to identify it. The Tag property helps you locate a control and can be used if you link a control to a data source. Tags also enclose controls when you work in design mode.

Properties also affect how the contents of a control are formatted, whether the control can be deleted, and whether its content can be edited. Other properties depend on the type of control you are working with. For example, for a plain-text control, you can set an option to allow multiple paragraphs.

Properties for the date picker control include the date format, the locale, and the calendar type.

You can set the date format and locale for a date picker content control.

The property Remove Content Control When Contents Are Edited can be set when you use a control to provide information about filling out information in the document, for example, but the content control is not needed when the document is completed and submitted. (This property is not available for every type of content control.)

Two properties you can set for controls help you protect the design and content of your document. The first property, Content Control Cannot Be Deleted, prevents a user of the document from deleting that control. You should set this property on every control that is required for the type of document you are creating. You can also set a property that prevents users from editing the content of a control. This property is suitable for titles or other controls whose content should remain static, such as text controls that display standardized text. Many controls require users to enter text, choose an option, or select an option from a list. For controls such as these, you should not set the option to prevent the content of a control from being edited.

In the Content Control Properties dialog box, by selecting Use A Style To Format Text Typed Into The Empty Control, you can apply a style to the content in a control. You can choose a style from the Style list (a limited number of styles are included) or click New Style in the Content Control Properties dialog box to open the Create New Style From Formatting dialog box.

See Also For information about creating styles, see "Objective 2.3: Create and manage styles."

If you are working with a combo box or list box content control, the Content Control Properties dialog box includes fields that you use to define list items. In the Add Choice dialog box, which Word displays when you click Add in the list properties area, you specify the display name and value for each list item.

In the Drop-Down List Properties area, set up and organize list or combo box items.

By default, Word repeats the text you enter in the Display Name box in the Value box (or vice versa, if you enter a value first). You can change the value to a numerical value, for example, to match a sequence of choices. Use the Modify button to make changes to the display names and values, and the Move Up and Move Down buttons to change the order of the items.

When you add content controls to a document, you can work in design mode. In design mode, Word displays tags that identify the content controls, and you can more easily arrange and edit the content controls in the document. When you insert a picture content control, however, you must turn off design mode before you can select the picture you want to display.

To turn design mode on or off

➜ On the **Developer** tab, in the **Controls** group, click the **Design Mode** button.

To insert a text content control

1. Click where you want to insert the control.

2. On the **Developer** tab, in the **Controls** group, click the **Rich Text Content Control** button or the **Plain Text Content Control** button.

To insert a picture content control

1. Click where you want to insert the control.

2. On the **Developer** tab, in the **Controls** group, click the **Picture Content Control** button.

3. If design mode is on, turn it off.

4. In the picture content control, click the icon to open the **Insert Pictures** window.

5. From the **Insert Pictures** window, locate and select the picture you want to display.

To insert a combo box or a drop-down list

1. Click where you want to insert the control.

2. On the **Developer** tab, in the **Controls** group, click the **Combo Box Content Control** button or the **Drop-Down List Content Control** button.

3. With the content control selected in the document, click **Properties** in the **Controls** group to open the **Content Control Properties** dialog box.

4. In the **Drop-Down List Properties** area, click **Add**.

5. In the **Add Choice** dialog box, enter the display name and value of the first list item that you want to appear in the content control, then click **OK**.

6. Repeat steps 4 and 5 to define each additional list item.

7. Select options for other properties, then click **OK**.

To insert a date picker content control

1. Click where you want to insert the date picker control.

2. On the **Developer** tab, in the **Controls** group, click the **Date Picker Content Control** button.

4

3. With the content control selected in the document, click **Properties** in the **Controls** group to open the **Content Control Properties** dialog box.

4. In the **Date Picker Properties** area, select the date format you want to use, and change the settings for the locale and calendar type if necessary.

To insert a check box content control

1. Click where you want to insert the check box control.

2. On the **Developer** tab, in the **Controls** group, click the **Check Box Content Control** button.

3. With the content control selected in the document, click **Properties** in the **Controls** group to open the **Content Control Properties** dialog box.

4. In the **Check Box Properties** area, click the **Change** button to open the **Symbol** dialog box to select a different symbol for a selected or cleared check box.

To insert a building block gallery content control

1. Click where you want to insert the control.

2. On the **Developer** tab, in the **Controls** group, click the **Building Block Gallery Content Control** button.

3. With the content control selected in the document, click **Properties** in the **Controls** group.

4. In the **Content Control Properties** dialog box, select the gallery and category of building blocks that you want to make available in the content control, then click **OK**.

To insert a repeating section content control

1. Select the content that you want to include in the control.

2. On the **Developer** tab, in the **Controls** group, click the **Repeating Section Content Control** button.

3. With the content control selected in the document, click **Properties** in the **Controls** group.

4. In the **Content Control Properties** dialog box, enter a section title, set other control properties, and then click **OK**.

To remove a content control from a document

→ Right-click the content control, then click **Remove Content Control**.

To customize the text in a content control

1. Turn on design mode.

2. Select the content control you want to edit.

3. Edit the placeholder text, and apply any formatting you want.

4. Turn off design mode.

To lock a control

1. Select the content control, and on the **Developer** tab, in the **Controls** group, click **Properties**.

2. In the **Content Control Properties** dialog box, in the **Locking** area, select one or both of the following, then click **OK**:

   • **Content control cannot be deleted**

   • **Contents cannot be edited**

To format a control

1. Select the content control, and on the **Developer** tab, in the **Controls** group, click **Properties**.

2. In the **Content Control Properties** dialog box, select the **Use a style to format text typed into the empty control** check box.

3. Do either of the following:

   • In the **Style** list, click the existing style you want to apply to content in the control.

   • Click **New Style** to open the **Create New Style from Formatting** dialog box. Define the attributes of the style, then click **OK**.

4. In the **Content Control Properties** dialog box, click **OK**.

4

Manage fields and their properties

Word uses fields to manage elements such as indexes and tables of contents. Later in this topic, you'll work with merge fields, which are used to specify information included in a mail merge.

In cases like these, Word inserts fields and sets field properties based on options you select in the user interface. You can also insert fields on your own to display information or to control how elements such as a table of contents appears.

The Field dialog box lists fields in categories such as Date And Time, Document Automation, Document Information, Links And References, and User Information. Fields that display document properties, such as author, keywords, and title, are listed in the Document Information category. You can display all fields or only the fields in a particular category.

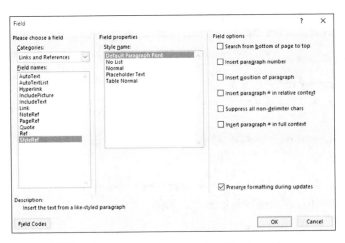

Set up a field by using the properties and options Word provides.

When you select a field in the Field dialog box, a list of the field's properties is displayed. Field properties often control formatting—for example, whether the text displayed by a field is in all uppercase characters or which numbering or date format a field's data will use. Field properties also identify information such as which style to associate with the StyleRef field or the data source that's linked to the Database field.

Clicking the Field Codes button changes the display in the dialog box so that you see the field code. The field code includes the field's name (such as FileSize) and can also include properties and other switches that affect how the field's data is formatted and what the field displays. (The term *switch* refers generally to both field properties and options.) For example, the field code {FILESIZE * CardNumber \k * MERGEFORMAT} shows a document's file size as a cardinal number in kilobytes. The MERGEFORMAT switch indicates that the field's format remains the same when it is updated.

In a document, you can view the output of the field or the field code itself. When the information displayed in a field changes, you can update the field so that it's current. Word also provides keyboard shortcuts you can use to manage fields in a document, as shown in the following table.

Keyboard shortcut	Action
Ctrl+F9	Inserts a blank field
Alt+F9	Switches the view between field codes and field output for all fields in the document
Shift+F9	Switches the view between field codes and field output for selected fields
F9	Updates selected fields
F11 or Shift+F11	Moves to the next or previous field
Ctrl+F11	Locks a field and prevents it from being updated
Ctrl+Shift+F11	Unlocks a field

Tip Click the Help button in the Field dialog box to display a support page that provides a reference of field codes, properties, and options.

The Field dialog box provides access to the properties that control what information a field displays and how the field displays it. For document information fields such as Author, Keywords, and Title, you can select the Uppercase, Lowercase, First Capital, or Title Case property to specify how the text displayed by these fields appears. In the category Links And References, the properties for the StyleRef field is the list of styles in the document. You select the style that's associated with the text you want the field to display (a section heading in a document's footer, for example).

Selecting a property in the Field Properties area of the Field dialog box adds that property to the field code. You can modify the properties used with a field by displaying the field code and then opening the Field Options dialog box. Depending on the field you are working with, the Field Options dialog box provides a list of formatting options, general switches (which are also often related to the format in which a field displays data), and any field-specific switches (which are not included for every field).

Keep in mind that some properties are not compatible with all fields or with other properties that field includes. You cannot, for example, apply a number format to text or add properties for two date formats to a single instance of a field.

Use general and field-specific switches to modify a field's data and format.

After you insert a field in a document, you can modify its properties by opening the Field dialog box from the menu displayed when you right-click the field.

To insert a field

1. On the **Insert** tab, in the **Text** group, click **Quick Parts**, then click **Field**.

2. In the **Field** dialog box, select the field you want to insert. Use the **Categories** list to view a subset of the fields.

3. In the **Field properties** area, select properties to format the field's data or to identify the source (such as a style name, a file name, or an image file) for the field's data.

4. In the **Field options** area, select the options you want to use with the field.

5. To view the elements of the field code, click **Field Codes**.

6. Click **Options** to open the **Field Options** dialog box, then select the properties and switches you want to apply.

7. Click **OK** in the **Field Options** dialog box, then click **OK** in the **Field** dialog box.

To modify field properties

1. In the **Field** dialog box, filter by category if necessary, and then in the **Field names** list, select the field you want to use.

2. If the property you want to apply is available in the **Field properties** area, click it. If the property isn't available in the **Field properties** area, do the following:

    Click the **Field Codes** button, then click the **Options** button.

    In the **Field Options** dialog box, select a property you want to apply to the field.

    Click **Add to Field**, then click **OK**.

To update a field

➜ Select the field, then press **F9**.

4

Objective 4.1 practice tasks

The practice files for these tasks are located in the **MOSWordExpert2019\ Objective4** practice file folder. The folder also contains result files that you can use to check your work.

➤ Open the **WordExpert_4-1a** document, and do the following:

- ❑ Under the existing text, add two plain-text content controls. Label the controls **Name** and **Email Address**.

- ❑ Under the plain-text controls, add a rich-text control. Label the control **Shipping Address**.

- ❑ Under the rich-text control, add a drop-down list content control that contains the list items **Small**, **Medium**, **Large**, and **Extra Large**. Label the drop-down list control **Jersey Size**.

- ❑ Under the drop-down list control, add a check box control. Label the control **Yes, send me your email newsletter**.

- ❑ To the right of the **Name** plain-text control, add a date picker content control. Label the control **Preferred Ship Date**.

➤ Save the **WordExpert_4-1a** document. Open the **WordExpert_4-1a_results** document. Compare the two documents to check your work. Then close the open documents.

➤ Open the **WordExpert_4-1b** document, and do the following:

- ❑ In the header, position the insertion point after the "Number of words in this document:" text, then insert a NumWords field using the default options.

- ❑ Close the header.

❏ Create a new paragraph and type the text *This sentence is not six words long, but nine.*

❏ Update the NumWords field in the header.

➤ Save the **WordExpert_4-1b** document. Open the **WordExpert_4-1b_results** document. Compare the two documents to check your work. Then close the open documents.

Objective 4.2: Create and modify macros

A *macro* is a series of tasks that you want Word to perform. In that sense, a macro is not unlike a recipe, which is a set of instructions that tells you what tasks to perform to cook or bake something. A macro, too, is a set of instructions, but it tells Word what tasks to perform to accomplish some goal.

The big difference is that a macro combines all these instructions into a single script—called a *procedure*—that you can invoke with a keystroke or just a few mouse clicks. In this sense, then, a macro isn't so much like a recipe for, say, how to bake bread, but is more akin to a bread machine, which, after it has been loaded with ingredients, bakes a loaf with the push of a button.

This list of instructions is composed mostly of macro statements. Some of these statements perform specific macro-related tasks, but most correspond to Word's commands and dialog box options. For example, you can close Word's current (active) window by selecting the File menu's Close command. In a VBA macro, the following statement does the same thing:

ActiveWindow.Close

This macro closes Word's active window.

Exam Strategy The objective domain for Exam MO-101, "Microsoft Word Expert (Word and Word 2019)," requires you to demonstrate the ability to record and edit simple macros. You will not be required to learn VBA or to create more complex procedures using the VBA Editor.

Record simple macros

Word lets you create a VBA macro automatically by recording a set of steps you perform in the program. With this method, you start the macro recording feature and then run through the operations you want to automate—which can include selecting text, running commands from the ribbon, and choosing dialog box options. The macro recorder takes note of each task you perform, translates everything into the appropriate VBA programming statements, and stores them where you can easily rerun the macro later on.

IMPORTANT While you record a macro, you can use the mouse to invoke commands but not to select objects, because selecting an object with the mouse isn't a step that Word can re-create.

The first step in recording a macro is to specify settings for the macro, including a name and a location. You can save a macro in *Normal.dotm*, which makes the macro available in all documents, or in the template file that is attached to the current document. You can assign a macro to a keyboard shortcut or to a button that you can place on the Quick Access Toolbar or on the ribbon.

Before you record a macro, it can be helpful to rehearse the steps you want to record. As an example, you might record a macro that applies a set of page-layout options, such as inserting a section break and setting the margins, page orientation, and header for the section. You could run a macro such as this in documents whose content requires pages that use the Landscape orientation (to display a wide table, for example) in addition to pages that retain the Portrait orientation. As preparation for recording the macro, walk through the options that you want to apply and the sequence in which you want to apply them.

You can take your time performing the actions while recording the macro because Word doesn't record the timing. You can pause recording when you need to determine which command or option to select next or to modify a setting that you have already selected. When you pause recording, you can effectively edit the macro (so that it applies the correct setting) without having to work directly with the VBA code that is generated by Word.

4

To open the Record Macro dialog box

→ On the **View** tab, in the **Macros** group, click **Record Macro**.

→ On the **Developer** tab, in the **Code** group, click **Record Macro**.

→ On the status bar, click the **Macro Recording** button.

Tip The Developer tab is hidden by default. You display the Developer tab from the Customize Ribbon page of the Word Options dialog box. For information about accessing hidden tabs, see "Display hidden ribbon tabs" in "Objective 1.1: Manage documents and templates."

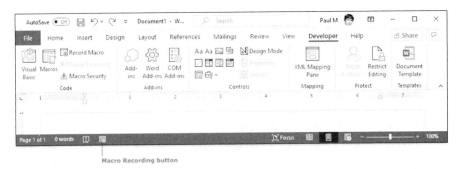

Macro Recording button

To get a recording started, click either Record Macro or Macro Recording.

To record a macro

1. Open the **Record Macro** dialog box.

2. In the **Macro name** box, enter a descriptive name for the macro following these rules and conventions:

   - Macro names must be no longer than 255 characters.

   - Names can contain numbers, but the first letter must be either a letter or an underscore (_).

   - Names cannot contain spaces or periods.

- If a macro name consists of multiple words, you can use underscores to separate the words. Alternatively, you can capitalize the first letter of each word.

Tip You learn later in this section that one way to run a recorded macro is to select it from a list of all your recorded macros. If you create many macros this way, that list will get quite long. Therefore, when naming your recorded macros, make sure you assign names that will make it easy to differentiate one macro from another. Names such as *Macro1* and *Macro2* tell you nothing, but names such as *AdjustWindowSize* and *NewDocumentTasks* are instantly understandable.

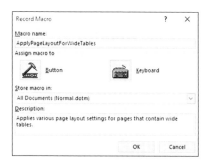

Give macros names that describe their purposes.

3. In the **Store macro in** list, select the template or document in which you want to save the macro.

Tip It is usually best to store macros using the default All Documents (*Normal.dotm*) option. This saves the macro in the Normal template, which makes it available to all open documents. You can also store the macro in any open template, which makes the macro available to any document that uses the template, or in any open document, which makes the macro available only to that document.

4. If you want to save a description of the macro, enter it in the **Description** box.

4

5. Click **OK**, and then perform the steps you want to record in the macro. Note that Word gives you two indications that a recording is in progress:

- The mouse pointer includes what looks like a cassette tape icon.
- The status bar's **Macro Recording** button changes to a blue square.

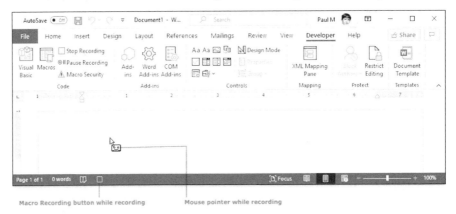

To get a recording started, click either Record Macro or Macro Recording.

6. When you are done, stop the recording, as described later in this task.

To pause and resume recording

1. On the **View** tab, in the **Macros** group, click **Pause Recording**. Alternatively, on the **Developer** tab, in the **Code** group, click **Pause Recording**.

2. Correct the previous settings or determine the next action to take.

3. On the **View** tab, in the **Macros** group, click **Resume Recording**. Alternatively, on the **Developer** tab, in the **Code** group, click **Resume Recording**.

To stop recording

→ On the **View** tab, in the **Macros** group, click **Stop Recording**.

→ On the **Developer** tab, in the **Code** group, click **Stop Recording**.

→ On the status bar, click the **Macro Recording** button.

Edit simple macros

You can edit a macro that you have recorded by opening the Visual Basic for Applications editor and code window. In the code window, you might change the font color the macro applies, for example, or change the text that is used in a find-and-replace operation you performed when you recorded the macro.

To open the Macros dialog box

→ On the **View** tab, in the **Macros** group, click **View Macros**.

→ On the **Developer** tab, in the **Code** group, click **Macros**.

To edit a macro

1. Open the **Macros** dialog box.

2. In the list of macros, select the macro you want to change, then click **Edit** to open the **Visual Basic for Applications** code window.

3. In the code window, edit the code statement you want to change.

4. Close the code window, then close the **Visual Basic for Applications** window.

Copy macros to other documents or templates

The macros that you create in one document or template can be copied so that you can use them in others. You use the Organizer to copy macros between documents and templates. This is done on the Macro Project Items tab of the dialog box, which has buttons and list boxes that you can use to open the template or document that contains the macros you want to copy and the template or document you want to copy the macros to.

IMPORTANT You cannot copy individual macro procedures from one document or template to another. Instead, Word only lets you copy collections of macros, which are called modules— although, in the Organizer, Word calls them *macro project items*.

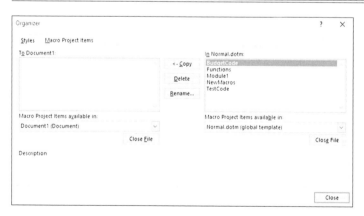

Copy a macro from one document or template to another.

To copy macros between documents or templates

1. On the **View** tab, in the **Macros** group, click the **Macros** arrow, then click **View Macros**.

2. In the **Macros** dialog box, click **Organizer** to display the **Macro Project Items** tab of the Organizer.

3. In the **Macro Project Items available in** lists, click the documents or templates you want to copy macros from and to. If the document or template isn't in the list, do the following:

    Click **Close File** to release the current macro list, then click **Open File** to display the content of the Templates folder.

    In the **Open** dialog box, navigate to and select the template or document you want to use, then click **Open**.

4. In the list box for the file you are copying macros from, select a macro or macros, then click **Copy**.

5. When you are done copying macros, click **Close**.

Objective 4.2 practice tasks

The practice file for these tasks is located in the **MOSWordExpert2019\
Objective4** practice file folder. The folder also contains a result file that you
can use to check your work.

➤ Open the **WordExpert_4-2** document, place the cursor at the end of
the document, and then record a macro named *PageSetup*—stored
in the **WordExpert_4-2** document—that does the following:

❏ Inserts a Next Page section break.

❏ Sets the page orientation of the new section to Landscape.

❏ Immediately after the section break, adds the text *Financial Results*,
styled as *Heading 1*.

❏ Below the *Financial Results* heading, inserts a table that has four
columns and four rows.

❏ Adds column headings to the table for *Quarter 1*, *Quarter 2*,
Quarter 3, and *Quarter 4*.

➤ Use the VBA Editor to edit the *PageSetup* macro to change the
inserted text from "Financial Results" to *Financial Results By Quarter*.

➤ Save the **WordExpert_4-2** document. Open the
WordExpert_4-2_results document. Compare the two
documents to check your work. Then close the open documents.

Objective 4.3: Perform mail merges

Form letters serve exceedingly useful purposes. If you're a business owner, a club offi-cer, or an information gatherer, form letters let you produce volumes of documents that are tailored to specific groups of people and that are personalized for individuals within those groups. Using Word, you can create form letters that are highly specific, both to your reader and to you. Word avoids the use of the unsavory term "form letter" and calls its form-letter-creation process *mail merge*.

Mail merge involves merging data, such as names and addresses, to create various kinds of mailings. The process involves the following three file types:

- **Data source** Holds the information about people that you add to your mailing. A table typically forms the data source.

- **Starting document** Provides both the common text and images as well as the merge fields into which Word adds personalized information.

- **Merge results** Individual letters or documents that reflect the merging of the data with the starting document.

Viewing the results of a successful mail-merge operation can be very satisfying. After some preliminary work on your part—creating the document you want to send and identifying information about the document's recipients—Word takes over, merges the content and information you supply, and produces each document you need. You can incorporate additional options to control how Word produces the documents, and you aren't limited to producing paper mailings—you can send a personal email message to each recipient in a group by using the mail-merge features in Word.

Setting up and running a mail-merge operation entails six general steps:

1. Open the starting document you want to use in the mail-merge operation and add text, illustrations, and other content as needed.

2. Specify the type of mail-merge output you want to create—a letter, email message, envelope, sheet of labels, directory, or Word document.

   > **Tip** A directory is like a catalog. It includes the same type of information about a group of items (for example, the name of each item, a description, and a price), but the information is distinct for each item.

3. Choose the data source that contains your recipient list and select the specific recipients you want.

4. Insert merge fields in the starting document. During the mail-merge operation, Word replaces the merge fields with information from the recipient list.

5. Preview the merge results. You can find specific recipients or move from record to record in the list. Word can also check for errors in advance and compile those errors in a separate document.

6. Merge the starting document and recipient list. You can edit and save individual documents, print the documents all at once, or send the documents as email messages.

Tip You can use the Step By Step Mail Merge Wizard to walk through the six mail-merge steps or perform them manually.

Manage recipient lists

Names, addresses, and other information you want to include about recipients in your mail-merge documents can come from a variety of sources. You can create an address list as a step in a mail-merge operation or use a list that's stored in a Microsoft Excel worksheet, a Microsoft Access database, your contacts list in Microsoft Outlook, or one of several other formats.

Tip To be of best use in a mail merge, the information in an external data source should be organized as you need to use it for recipient information. For example, if you are compiling an address list in Excel, it's best to include a header row with column names that correspond to the fields Word uses for addresses in a mail-merge operation (such as *First*, *Last*, *Company*, *Mobile_Phone*, and so on).

The Type A New List option on the Select Recipients menu opens the New Address List dialog box, where you can compile a recipient list for the mail-merge operation. After you build the list, Word saves it in MDB format. You can select this list for other mail-merge operations in the future.

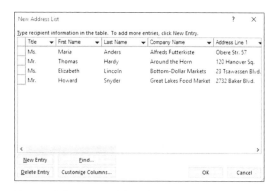

You can define your recipient data source directly in Word.

Scroll to the right in this dialog box to view the group of fields available by default. You can click the Customize Columns button to open a dialog box in which you can define additional fields, delete fields you don't need, rename fields, and change the order of the fields. By defining a custom field, you expand the type of information you can insert and display in a mail-merge operation. For example, you could create a field named **Donation** and enter the amount a recipient donated to your organization, or you could create a field named **Auction Item** and use it to describe what someone purchased at an auction. The amount of information you can store in a custom field is limited to 254 characters, including spaces.

In the New Address List dialog box, click a column heading to sort the list by that column, or click the arrow beside a column heading to open a menu to sort and filter the list in other ways. You can filter for a specific value, filter for blank values to fill in missing information, or click Advanced to open the Filter And Sort dialog box. On the Sort Records page in the Filter And Sort dialog box, you can specify as many as three fields to sort by. On the Filter Records page, you can set up a simple, single-field filter to find all records that equal (or do not equal) a specific value, or you can define multifield filters by using the OR and AND operators. Use the OR operator when you want to view records that match any of the conditions you define. Use the AND operator to select records that match both conditions you define.

The Comparison list on the Filter Records page includes the Less Than, Greater Than, Less Than Or Equal, Greater Than Or Equal, and other operators. You can use these operators to find records with specific numeric values in a custom field you create. For example, for a mail-merge operation related to a fundraising campaign, you could create and populate a custom field named **Pledge** or **Donation** and then filter on the values for that field (pledges above $1,000, for example) to send a document only to those recipients. For text fields such as names and locations (city or country/region, for example) or a field such as Zip Code, you can use the Contains or Does Not Contain operators to find recipients who live in a specific area or whose last name is Lambert.

You can filter and sort recipient lists by multiple criteria.

If you select an Excel workbook or an Access database as the source of a recipient list, Word opens the Select Table dialog box. This dialog box lists each worksheet and named range in an Excel workbook or the tables and queries defined in an Access database. In this dialog box, you can select the worksheet, range, or database object you want to use.

A Word document that contains nothing but a table is also a valid source of data for a recipient list. You can set up the table with the column headings you want to use for fields in the mail merge.

If the information you want to use for the recipient list is stored in a server database (for example, a Microsoft SQL Server database), you can use the Data Connection wizard to create a connection. As you step through the wizard, you need to provide information such as the server name and the user name and password required to gain access to the server. Choosing the Other/Advanced option in the wizard opens the Data Link Properties dialog box. In this dialog box, you select a data source provider and specify the information and other initialization properties required to make a connection. You might need to obtain some of this information from a network or server administrator.

If you maintain and manage a detailed contacts list in Outlook—including information such as company names, phone numbers, mailing addresses, and other details—you can make productive use of your contacts folder as the data source for a mail-merge operation. All the contacts in the folder you choose are selected for the operation by default.

4

Tip If you make changes to your Outlook contact list, click Refresh in the Mail Merge Recipients dialog box to update the list of recipients for the mail merge. Keep in mind that you cannot edit Outlook contact information while working in the Mail Merge Recipients dialog box.

To create and manage a recipient list

1. On the **Mailings** tab, in the **Start Mail Merge** group, click **Select Recipients**, then click **Type New List**.

2. In the **New Address List** dialog box, enter the information for the first recipient, then click **New Entry**.

3. Repeat step 2 to add the information for each recipient.

4. In the **New Address List** dialog box, click **OK**.

5. In the **Save Address List** dialog box, open the folder you want to save the recipient list in, then click **Save**.

To modify a recipient list

1. In the **New Address List** dialog box, click **Customize Columns**.

2. Do any of the following:

    - To add a custom field, click **Add,** enter the name of the field in the **Add Field** dialog box, and then click **OK**.

    - To change the order of the fields, select the field you want to move and then click **Move Up** or **Move Down**.

    - To locate a specific recipient in the list, click **Find**. In the **Find Entry** dialog box, enter the text string you want Word to find. This might be a first name, a last name, a city name, or a value related to a different field. To search for this text in a specific field, click **This Field** and then choose the field you want to search. Click **Find Next**. Click **Cancel** when you locate the field you are looking for.

    - To delete an entry, select the row, then click **Delete Entry**.

To select an external data source

1. On the **Mailings** tab, in the **Start Mail Merge** group, click **Select Recipients**, then click **Use an Existing List**.

2. In the **Select Data Source** dialog box, open the folder that contains the data source file you want to use.

    > **IMPORTANT** If the dialog box doesn't display the data source file, select the format or All Files (*.*) in the Files Of Type list.

3. Select the data source file, then click **Open**.

4. If the **Select Table** dialog box opens, choose the worksheet, cell range, or database object that contains the recipient information you want, then click **OK**.

To use an Outlook contact folder as a recipient list

1. On the **Mailings** tab, in the **Start Mail Merge** group, click **Select Recipients**, then click **Choose from Outlook Contacts**.

2. If prompted, choose the Outlook profile that is associated with the contacts folder you want to use.

3. In the **Select Contacts** dialog box, select the contacts folder you want to use, then click **OK**.

4. In the **Mail Merge Recipients** dialog box, clear the check box to the left of any contact you don't want to include in the mail merge.

5. If you want to refresh the list so that it shows recent changes made in Outlook, select **Contacts** in the **Data Source** pane, then click **Refresh**.

Modify recipient lists

After you choose a recipient list, you can edit or filter it to include only specific recipients, and sort it to set the order of the merged documents or labels. For example, you might want to sort by city or by company for a mailing you are preparing for specific clients or locales.

You can locate specific contacts or duplicate contacts within the recipient list. For certain types of data sources (such as Excel workbooks and Access databases, but not for Outlook contact lists), you can edit detailed information about recipients when the recipient list is displayed.

To edit a recipient list

1. On the **Mailings** tab, in the **Start Mail Merge** group, click **Edit Recipient List**.

2. In the **Mail Merge Recipients** dialog box, select the recipient list in the **Data Source** area, then click **Edit**.

3. In the **Edit Data Source** dialog box, update the values for fields, or click **New Entry** to add a recipient record.

4. In the **Edit Data Source** dialog box, click **OK**. In the message box Word displays, click **Yes** to update the recipient list and save the changes to the original data source.

4

To refine a recipient list

1. On the **Mailings** tab, in the **Start Mail Merge** group, click **Edit Recipient List**.

2. In the **Mail Merge Recipients** dialog box, do any of the following:

   - Use the arrows beside column headings to sort the list by that field (in ascending or descending order) or to filter the list by values in that field or for blank or nonblank fields.

   - For more advanced sorts, in the **Refine Recipient List** area, click **Sort** to open the **Filter and Sort** dialog box. On the **Sort Records** tab, you can sort by up to three fields.

   - To define an advanced filter, in the **Refine Recipient List** area, click **Filter**. On the **Filter Records** page of the **Filter and Sort** dialog box, select the field you want to filter by. Select a comparison operator, and then enter the text you want to use for the filter. In the far-left column, you can also select the AND or OR operator and then add another field to the filter. Repeat this step to define other conditions for the filter.

   - To check for duplicate recipients, click **Find Duplicates**. In the **Find Duplicates** dialog box, clear the check box beside the duplicate entries you don't want to include.

   - To locate a specific recipient, click **Find Recipient**. In the **Find Entry** dialog box, enter the text you want Word to search for. To search in a specific field, select **This Field**, then select the field you want to use.

3. In the **Mail Merge Recipients** dialog box, click **OK**.

Insert merge fields

Merge fields correspond to the columns of information in a recipient list. To add the information stored in a recipient list to a document, you insert merge fields where you want the information to appear in the document. You can place the information at the start of the document to define an address block or a greeting, and within the body of the document, where you might include a company name or other information.

Word provides composite merge fields for an address block and a greeting line. The Address Block command in the Write & Insert Fields group inserts standard information such as title, first and last names, mailing address, city, state, country/region, and postal code. In the Insert Address Block dialog box, you can tailor the address block so that it fits the needs of the mail-merge operation you have underway.

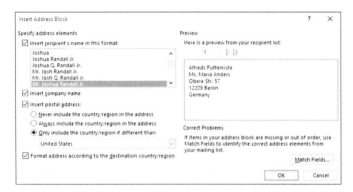

By default, address blocks include all possible elements.

The ways you can modify the standard address block include the following:

- Choose a format for recipient names (first name only, first and last names, first and last names with title, and others).

- Clear the Insert Company Name check box if you don't want to include that information. (The check box is selected by default.)

- Clear the Insert Postal Address check box. For example, you might want only names to appear in the document and use address information for labels or envelopes. You can also specify under what conditions you want the country/region name to appear in the address block.

The Greeting Line command presents similar kinds of options. You can alter the salutation from Dear to To, for example, and specify how recipient names appear. Use the Greeting Line For Invalid Recipient Names list to choose a greeting that Word applies when information in the recipient list doesn't match the format you choose for a name.

You add individual merge fields, including any custom fields you define when building a recipient list, to a document by choosing the fields from the Insert Merge Field list or by using the options in the Insert Merge Field dialog box. In the dialog box, the Address Fields option displays an extended list of fields. The Database Fields option displays the fields defined in the associated recipient list.

Insert merge fields from this dialog box to include recipient information in the mail merge.

You can insert merge fields at any place in the document that makes sense. For example, in the final paragraph of a letter, you might repeat the recipient's first name for emphasis—"In closing, I want to thank you again, <<First_Name>>, for your support of our campaign."

If the fields in an Excel worksheet or other data source you are using for recipient information don't correspond precisely with the fields in Word, use the Match Fields command in the Write & Insert Fields group to open a dialog box in which you can set up the field relationships you need. (You can also open this dialog box by clicking the Match Fields button in the Insert Address Block or Insert Greeting Line dialog box.) In the Match Fields dialog box, if a field in your data source doesn't match a field in Word, Word displays Not Matched. Keep in mind that you cannot include any unmatched fields in the mail-merge document. You can save the configuration of matching fields if you expect to use this data source for other mail-merge operations on the computer you are using.

Tip You don't need to complete a mail-merge operation in one sitting. You can save a document you are preparing for a mail-merge operation, and Word maintains the association with the data source for recipients and any merge fields you have inserted. When you open the document to begin work again, click Yes in the message box that Word displays to confirm that you want to open the document and run an SQL command.

The Preview Results command inserts recipient records into the merge fields so that you can see how each document will appear. You can use the Find Recipient command to locate a specific recipient, or use the preview arrows to move from record to record in the recipient list.

Word can check for errors before you print documents or run your mail merge via email. The dialog box that Word displays provides three options: simulating the merge and reporting errors in a new document, running the merge and pausing if Word encounters an error, and completing the merge and reporting errors in a separate document. The types of errors Word checks for include missing information in the recipient list.

To insert an address block merge field

1. In the document, click where you want to insert the address block.

2. On the **Mailings** tab, in the **Write & Insert Fields** group, click **Address Block**.

3. In the **Insert Address Block** dialog box, do any of the following:

   - In the **Insert recipient's name in this format** pane, click the format you want to use for recipient names.

   - To exclude names from the address block, clear the **Insert recipient's name in this format** check box.

   - To exclude the company name or postal address, clear the corresponding check box.

   - If you include the postal address, select an option for when to include the country/region name in the address block.

   - If you want to use the same format for all addresses, clear the **Format address according to the destination country/region** check box.

4. In the **Preview** area, review the effect of your choices on the content and structure of the addresses.

To insert a greeting line merge field

1. In the document, click where you want to insert the greeting line.

2. On the **Mailings** tab, in the **Write & Insert Fields** group, click **Greeting Line**.

4

3. In the **Insert Greeting Line** dialog box, do either of the following:

- Specify a format for the elements of the greeting line, including the salutation and name format.

- Choose a format for invalid recipient names.

4. In the **Preview** area, review the effect of your choices on the content and structure of the greeting line.

To insert a merge field

1. In the document, click where you want to insert the merge field.

2. On the **Mailings** tab, in the **Write & Insert Fields** group, do either of the following:

- Click the **Insert Merge Field** arrow, then click the field you want to insert.

- Click the **Insert Merge Field** button. In the **Insert Merge Field** dialog box, click the field you want to insert, then click **Insert**.

To match merge fields with recipient list fields

1. On the **Mailings** tab, in the **Write & Insert Fields** group, click **Match Fields**.

2. In the **Match Fields** dialog box, in the list on the right, select a field from your recipient list to match the field names Word provides in the list on the left.

Use this dialog box to match fields in your recipient list with merge fields in Word.

3. Click **OK**.

To preview mail-merge results

1. On the **Mailings** tab, in the **Preview Results** group, click **Preview Results**.

2. In the **Preview Results** group, do any of the following:

   • Click the arrows to show the first, next, previous, or last mail-merge record.

   • Click **Find Recipient**. In the **Find Record** dialog box, enter the text you want to search for, then click **Find Next**.

   • Click **Check for Errors**, then select the option you want to use.

Add mail-merge rules

Mail-merge rules enable you to define conditional elements that can add flexibility and help customize records produced in a mail-merge operation. The rules are listed on the Rules menu in the Write & Insert Fields group.

One helpful rule is the If Then Else rule. With this rule, you can specify an IF condition (for example, "If the State field is equal to California") and then enter the text you want Word to insert when the condition you define is true and alternative text that Word inserts when the IF condition is false.

You can set up mail-merge rules to customize content based on conditions you define.

Two other rules you might make use of are Ask and Fill In. These rules can prompt you as each mail-merge document is produced so that you can change information on the fly. You set up an Ask rule to prompt you or another user to enter text at a specific location. The Ask rule uses a bookmark you create to mark the location in the document. For example, you might create a bookmark named **Discount** where you want to specify the discount that a customer is going to receive. You can then enter a prompt that lets you or another user know what text to enter. You can also define the text you want to display by default. In the Insert Word Field: Ask dialog box, you can select the Ask Once check box if you want to be prompted only at the start of the final mail merge. Keep the check box cleared if you want the prompt to appear for each record. When you start merging documents, you'll be prompted to accept the default text or insert an alternative for the document being produced. The Fill-In rule works similarly.

To define an If Then Else mail-merge rule

1. On the **Mailings** tab, in the **Write & Insert Fields** group, click **Rules**, and then click **If...Then...Else....**

2. In the **Insert Word Field: IF** dialog box, do the following and then click **OK**:

   In the **Field name** list, select the field you want to use in an IF condition.

   In the **Comparison** list, select a comparison operator.

   In the **Compare to** box, enter the text or other value you want to compare the field with.

   In the **Insert this text** box, enter the text that you want Word to insert when the IF condition is true.

   In the **Otherwise insert this text** box, enter the text that should appear when the condition you define is false.

Send email messages to groups of recipients

If you have a compatible email program (Outlook, for example), you can set up a mail-merge operation to send an email message to a list of recipients. Each message is a single item addressed to a single recipient—the message isn't sent to the group as a whole—and you can personalize each message as you might a mail-merge document by using, for example, only a first name.

One key in sending email messages is that your data source should include a column labeled E-Mail Address in the header row. Set up the document with an address block, greeting line, and other merge fields as you would for a printed letter. You can then preview the results of each message you plan to send.

To send an email message as a mail-merge document

1. Create the document you want to send as an email message.

2. Select or build the recipient list, insert merge fields, and define merge rules as necessary.

3. On the **Mailings** tab, in the **Finish** group, click **Finish & Merge**, then click **Send Email Messages**.

4. In the **Merge to E-mail** dialog box, do the following and then click **OK**:

   In the **To** list, select the field that contains the recipients' email addresses.

   In the **Subject line** box, enter the text that you want to appear in the message subject field.

   In the **Message format** list, click **Attachment**, **Plain text**, or **HTML**.

   In the **Send records** area, select the recipient records you want to send the message to.

Configure label or envelope settings for mail-merge operations

The Mailings tab provides a couple of ways to configure settings for labels and envelopes and then print on them. You can use the Envelopes or Labels option on the Start Mail Merge menu to merge information from your recipient list to produce the envelope or label setup you need. You can use the Envelopes and Labels commands in the Create group (at the far left of the Mailings tab) to prepare and print these items without setting up a full mail-merge operation.

When you are preparing to print on labels or envelopes as part of a mail-merge operation, start with a blank document. If you have a document open when you select either option from the Start Mail Merge menu, Word displays a warning telling you that it must delete the contents of the open document and discard any changes before it can continue.

Depending on the options you select for envelopes or labels (envelope size, for example, or label vendor and product number), Word displays a document with an area in which you insert merge fields. You can enter or select a recipient list, and then add the merge fields you want to include on the envelopes or labels. You can use the Address Block command, for example, or add individual merge fields. You can also add merge rules. For example, you might add the Merge Record # rule as a way to determine how many labels or envelopes you print.

With merge fields in place, you can preview the results and then use the Finish & Merge menu to print on the labels or envelopes.

4

To configure and print on envelopes

1. Start with a blank document.

2. On the **Start Mail Merge** menu, click **Envelopes**.

3. In the **Envelope Options** dialog box, do the following and then click **OK**:

    Select the envelope size.

    Change the font formatting for the addresses as needed.

    On the **Printing Options** tab, check that the settings are correct for the printer you are using.

4. Click **Select Recipients**, then choose an option for the recipient list you want to use.

5. Add merge fields to the envelope to create an address block.

6. Preview the results, and check for any errors.

7. Click **Finish & Merge**, then click **Print Documents**.

To configure and print on labels

1. Start with a blank document.

2. On the **Start Mail Merge** menu, click **Labels**.

3. In the **Label Options** dialog box, do the following and then click **OK**:

    Select the type of printer you are using.

    In the **Label Information** area, select the label vendor and then the product number for the label you are using.

4. Click **Select Recipients**, then choose an option for the recipient list you want to use.

5. Add merge fields to the document to create an address block.

6. Preview the results, and check for any errors.

7. Click **Finish & Merge**, then click **Print Documents**.

Objective 4.3 practice tasks

The practice file for these tasks is located in the **MOSWordExpert2019\ Objective4** practice file folder. The folder also contains a result file that you can use to check your work.

➤ Open the **WordExpert_4-3** document and do the following:

❑ Choose the option to use an existing list as the recipient list. Select the **WordExpert_4-3** workbook.

❑ Use the Match Fields command to match the *Role* field to the *Job Title* field.

❑ Insert an address block at the top of the document. Insert the *First Name* field after the opening salutation.

❑ Insert a greeting line below the address block. Insert the *First Name* field after the opening salutation.

❑ Replace the *JOBTITLE* placeholder with the *Role* field.

❑ Replace the *SALES* placeholder with the *Sales* field.

❑ Replace the *SUPERVISOR* placeholder with the *Supervisor* field.

❑ Create an If Then Else merge rule for the *Sales* field that inserts the text **exceeded the goal. Nice work!** for the records in which the sales is greater than or equal to $100,000. For other records, use the text **did not reach the goal. Keep trying!**. (Be sure to add a space at the start of the text to separate the text from the field.)

❑ Preview the records.

➤ Save the **WordExpert_4-3** document. Open the **WordExpert_4-3_results** document. Compare the two documents to check your work. Then close the open documents.

Index

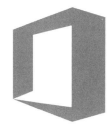

Plug into learning at

MicrosoftPressStore.com

The Microsoft Press Store by Pearson offers:

- Free U.S. shipping

- Buy an eBook, get three formats – Includes PDF, EPUB, and MOBI to use with your computer, tablet, and mobile devices

- Print & eBook Best Value Packs

- eBook Deal of the Week – Save up to 50% on featured title

- Newsletter – Be the first to hear about new releases, announcements, special offers, and more

- Register your book – Find companion files, errata, and product updates, plus receive a special coupon* to save on your next purchase

Discounts are applied to the list price of a product. Some products are not eligible to receive additional discounts, so your discount code may not be applied to all items in your cart. Discount codes cannot be applied to products that are already discounted, such as eBook Deal of the Week, eBooks that are part of a book + eBook pack, and products with special discounts applied as part of a promotional offering. Only one coupon can be used per order.